HEROES OF
THE RAF

GUY GIBSON vc

John Fareham

Bretwalda Books Ltd

To my father, **Squadron Leader J.L. Fareham C. Eng, M.R.Ae.S** *who took the King's shilling and never approved of my career choice of public service but still supported me – I hope this makes amends for the many arguments we had about this career choice of public service when I was younger*

To my mother **Christine Fareham,** *who took the King's sixpence, as she put it, but kept the peace*

To **A.M.S.** *another mistake of my callow youth I hope to put right "If in the twilight of memory we should meet once more, we shall speak again together and you shall sing to me a deeper song".*

First Published 2012
Text Copyright © John Fareham 2012

All rights reserved. No reproduction of any part of this publication is permitted without the prior written permission of the publisher:

Bretwalda Books
Unit 8, Fir Tree Close, Epsom,
Surrey KT17 3LD

info@BretwaldaBooks.com

www.BretwaldaBooks.com

To receive an e-catalogue of our complete range of books send an email to
info@BretwaldaBooks.com

ISBN 978-1-907791-58-1

Bretwalda Books Ltd

Foreword

*I have enjoyed writing this book despite the
frustrations inherent in establishing facts. Ignoring a
tendency on the internet for people
to publish opinions as facts.*

*It seems that, despite my main period of interest being
the Napoleonic Wars to the outbreak of World War I,
in many ways I was inevitably going to write this
book. My Father flew Bombers and I grew up on
more draughty isolated RAF bases than I can
comfortably recall. Guy Gibson was always a
boyhood hero of mine, I saw the film early and found
a Pan paperback of "Enemy Coast Ahead" which I
read under the covers at night it was so enthralling
and it is a delight that researching him has not
changed my opinion. The RAF is a small world,
many of the places in this story I knew: I was born in
RAF St Athan, in Glamorgan and now live a short
hop away from Scampton and Hemswell, places
integral to Gibson's life, bizarrely at one point I even
lived, briefly in Munchen-Gladbach.*

John Fareham

An Imperial
Childhood

P erhaps fittingly for a man who would become known to some as "The Boy Emperor", Guy Penrose Gibson was born in Simla, the summer capital of the British Raj, in the India of the King Emperor. Entering this world on 12th August 1918 Guy was the son of Alexander James Gibson and Leonora Mary, nee Strike.

It was not atypical in the Imperial days for a man to establish his career before marriage. Alexander Gibson, born 14th May 1877 in Russia, was the son of Charles John and Elizabeth Gibson. Alexander had entered the Indian

VICE REGAL LODGE SIMLA
The city of Simla (now Shimla) stands 7,000 feet up in the foothills of the western Himalayas. At the time that Gibson was born here Simla was the favoured summer resort for British families escaping the heat of the plains.

Forestry Service, founded in part through the activities of his ancestor, another Alexander Gibson, who had been born in Scotland in 1800 becoming, in 1843, the first conservator of the new Forestry Service.

Leaves taken in Britain were the norm for Imperial workers to see "the Home Country" and so it was that Alexander Gibson took a holiday at Porthleven in Cornwall. Returning from her education in a Belgian Convent in 1913 Leonora Mary Strike, generally known as Nora, and Alexander Gibson met each other. Nora's family home was on the cliffs on the north side of Porthleven. Nora was one of several daughters of Captain Edward Carter Strike of the Hain Steamship Company, and Emily Jane, nee Symons. In October 1913, once Nora had turned nineteen Alexander proposed and

PORTHLEVEN HARBOUR
Gibson's mother, Nora Strike, lived in Porthleven, Cornwall. It was here that the 18 year old Nora met Gibson's father when the latter was on holiday in 1913. The young couple married in the village later that year, then left for India.

was accepted. A month later Alexander and Nora married at Porthleven Wesleyan Chapel, on 2nd December, and left for India.

Nora gave birth to a son, Alexander Edward Charles on 23rd June 1915; a daughter Joan on 10th August 1916; and finally another son, Guy, born on 12th August 1918 and christened on 11th September. However, long-term domestic life in India was not always an option for young families in the Empire. Many imperial workers wanted their children educated in England and so it was that Alexander Edward went to St George's Preparatory School in Folkestone. The other Gibson children and their mother also returned to England in 1924, Alexander senior staying in India until 1929 when he retired from service in India.

On their return to Cornwall, Guy was sent to school locally with his sister until he was old enough to follow his brother to St George's where he stayed until 1932. Guy then moved on to St Edwards School on the Woodstock Road, Oxford, where again he joined his brother.

Guy's contemporaries recall him as showing much determination and being immensely energetic at games. His housemaster Freddie Yorke was later to recall Gibson as "strong minded without obstinacy, disarmingly frank, and of great charm". The exigencies of the parental Gibson's lives meant sometimes Guy, and his brother, used to stay with Yorke during some of the holidays. Guy was an enthusiastic cricketer, and earned his House Colours for a determined stand of some 160 runs as the inter-House underdogs. He was also a competent rugger player, but did not make the first team. Guy was recalled as a boy "devoid of nastiness", good-natured and a great "joiner-in". Gibson became a House Prefect and gained a good-natured and easy-going reputation not being unduly concerned with petty discipline. Gibson was also a Corporal in the School Officer Training Corps.

Nobody records or recalls Gibson's academic achievements as exemplary. Recalled as interested in science, mechanics and speed, Gibson also had an artistic streak with an interest in pantomimes, music, plays, and photography – although he himself was later to comment, "Well I'm not a highbrow by any means". Nevertheless, Gibson took his school exams and obtained his Oxford and Cambridge School Certificate with credits in English, Latin, History, French (oral), with Physics and Chemistry combined.

Gibson had decided he wanted to be a Test Pilot. In August 1936 entered the RAF solely in order to learn to fly, but with no intention of a long term

RAF UXBRIDGE OFFICERS' MESS
In the interwar years, RAF Uxbridge was a major administrative centre for the air force, hosting among other organisations the RAF School of Music, Headquarters Southern Area, Southern Area Medical Headquarters, Southern Area Barrack Stores, and the Headquarters of the Air Construction Service.

career there. Gibson was sent to Yatesbury, Wiltshire, where the Bristol Aeroplane Company was running a new training school for the RAF. Gibson arrived on 16th November 1936, along with 33 others, becoming part of No.6 Course. Despite a week's extension to the course because of poor weather the pupil intake nevertheless failed to complete the 50 hours of flying expected. Even so, on 31st January 1937, Gibson still succeeded in leaving Yatesbury as an Acting Pilot Officer - one of 28 who passed the course.

Pausing for a brief period at 24 Training Group Depot, RAF Uxbridge, to familiarise himself with King's Regulations, Drill and other minutiae of service life; on 6th February Acting P/O Gibson went to No.6 F.T.S (Flying Training School) at Netheravon becoming part of No.5 course. Gibson, and other successful pupils of No.5 Course, were authorised to receive their Flying Badge on 24th May, w.e.f. 22nd May. This phase of Gibson's life concluded when No.5 Course had their passing out parade, on 31st August 1937, presided over by Air Vice Marshal Pattinson the A.O.C. No.23 (Training) Group.

Off to War

In common with the rest of No.5 Course, all with their flying training completed, Acting Pilot Officer Guy Penrose Gibson received a posting to an operational unit. In Gibson's case the posting was to No.83 Squadron, flying Hawker Hinds out of RAF Turnhouse on 4th September 1937. RAF Turnhouse, some seven miles west of Edinburgh, was also home to No.603, City of Edinburgh Squadron, an Auxiliary Air Force Unit flying Hawker Fury fighters. Turnhouse now forms, in part, Edinburgh Airport.

The Hawker Hind biplane bomber had entered squadron service at the start of 1937. Powered by a Kestrel engine the Hind had a top speed of 186 mph at 16,400 feet, a range of 430 miles, and could carry a bomb load of

HAWKER HIND
Gibson went operational with the RAF on the Hawker Hind, one of the better biplane bombers of the interwar years. The RAF would move its Hinds to a training role before the war began, though South African Hinds fought Italian colonial forces in Africa in 1941.

500 lb. At this date the Hind was the most important light bomber in RAF service, though it was soon to be superseded by the monoplane Fairey Battle and Bristol Blenheim which were already entering service in 1937.

Assigned to 'A' Flight, Gibson trained, engaged in stunts and japes, explored his ability and that of the machine - as most young pilots did - and early showed a preference for some low level flying. Gibson was duly confirmed as a Pilot Officer in November 1937. The following March, No.83 Squadron moved to Scampton in Lincolnshire. At this date, RAF Bomber Command was organised into a number of Groups, each consisting of a number of stations and up to seven squadrons. Scampton, and so No.83 Squadron, lay within 5 Group.

Arguably the highest profile bomber airfield in Britain, Scampton, grew out of a World War I airfield known as Brattlesby Cliff or Brattlesby, five miles north of Lincoln. It had closed after peace came in 1918, but reopened in 1935 as a reaction to increasing German militarism. In October 1938, No.83 Squadron discarded its Hinds in favour of the Handley Page Hampden. As was usual, the Squadron's strength was 16 Hampdens with five in reserve.

The Hampden was a twin-engined, twin-tailed, aircraft with a maximum speed of 265 miles per hour at 15,000 feet and a service ceiling of 19,000 feet. Carrying their maximum bomb-load of 11,780 lbs the Hampden had a range of 1,095 miles. The Hampden's weakness later proved to be a lack of

BRISTOL BLENHEIM
A Bristol Blenheim bomber circles a burning enemy ship in the early months of the war. The Blenheim was one of the first RAF aircraft to have an all-metal stressed-skin construction with fully retractable landing gear, flaps and variable pitch propellers. Designed to be a fast bomber, it was later used as a nightfighter.

defensive armament. There was a forward firing machine gun and a pair of guns on a scarf ring facing backward over the fuselage. Two more guns were later added in the belly behind the bomb bay. It was originally intended to have a powered turret, but no turret manufactured at the time could fit the fuselage of the Hampden so the idea was dropped.

The limitations of the Hampden would not be clear until the war began. Meanwhile, the pilots were engaged in learning the new machine and probably revelling in enclosed cockpits and retractable under-carriages. In the spring of 1939 No.83 squadron was posted back to Scotland for armament practice, bomb-aiming and machine-gun firing. Gibson then went to Hamble in Hampshire for advanced navigational training, followed by a month at RAF Northolt for joint training with Fighter Command.

Gibson went on leave in late August 1939, but was abruptly recalled to Scampton on 1 September. That day the Germans invaded Poland, and two days later British Prime Minister Neville Chamberlain announced that Britain was again at war with Germany.

The first operational sortie of the war began with a Bristol Blenheim piloted by F/O A.M. McPherson and crew, from No 139 Squadron based at Wyton, Cambridgeshire. McPherson carried out a photographic reconnaissance of the German naval base at Wilhelmshaven, taking off just after mid-day. As a result, the RAF formed a bomber force of 18 Hampdens from 5 Group. The Operational Record Book (ORB) at Scampton recording "One raid of 9 aircraft carried out, consisting of one sub-formation of 49 Squadron, 2 sub-formations of No.83 Squadron"; to be followed into the attack by nine Wellingtons from No.3 Group.

Gibson was one of those from No.83 Squadron to take part in this, the first RAF bombing raid of the war. The instructions were "Aircraft are to sweep south from VORNEES LIGHTSHIP". The time over the target ordered "as early as possible after time of despatch" and the type of attack ordered as "low level bombing at high speed fore and aft from stern". The orders specified an alternative target of the ammunition dump at Mariensiel, also near Wilhelmshaven.

Gibson, whose "own head was on a swivel because I had heard from one or two chaps who fought in the last war that this was the only way to survive" spotted a German Dornier 17 flying about 500 feet below them. Whilst confessing his natural instinct to attack, Gibson showed he knew the

11

difference between heroism and rashness by staying on course. "It is written way back in the code of bomber rules," he later recalled, "that the bomber's job is to get to the target and back again, not to go doing any fancy stuff, and so we kept straight on".

The Squadron flew on as the cloud ceiling descended to 300 feet and the rain continued. With cloud at 100 feet, Leonard Snaith, C/O No.83 Squadron, decided to turn back. Although the Wellingtons had returned by 22:40, the Hampdens had no such luck. Crossing the British coast after dark their flight leader got lost because all the beacons were in code mode. The crews flew around the general area of what they believed to be Lincolnshire trying to find their position. When the moon rose the Hampden pilots became neither the first nor the last generation of pilots to be grateful for two great landmarks of Lincoln – the Cathedral and the canal. Spotting, in this case, the canal, No.83 Squadron managed to find their way home.

The so-called Phoney War lasted from the fall of Poland at the end of September 1939 to the German invasion of Denmark and Norway in April 1940. While there were some military actions during this time, there was no major offensive. For RAF Scampton, the ORB was to show no operations at all during the month of October; and Gibson himself was not to fly on another operation until 27th February 1940. Nevertheless, the fact remained that Guy Gibson had made his first operational mission, which had shown his pluck, positive attitude, determination to complete a mission without distraction; and of course he was 'blooded'. Gibson was blooded in another way when, he was bitten by the Station Commander's dog, a black Labrador called "Zimba". Given 36 hours leave Gibson was able to be Best Man at his brother's wedding to Ruth Harris in Rugby Parish Church.

Although the RAF did carry out some bombing raids during the Phoney War, the main activity was leaflet dropping. The commander of 5 Group at this date was Arthur Harris, later to become the commander of Bomber Command and to gain the nickname of "Bomber Harris". After the war, Harris described this activity as supplying "the continent's requirements of toilet paper for the five long years of the war". However, leaflet raids and reconnaissance flights helped improve RAF navigation and other skills – less helpfully, they aided the Germans in anti-aircraft preparation as the Germans anticipated shifts from pamphlets to explosives!

Although some in No.83 Squadron did more offensive operations, often anti-naval patrols, Gibson was not one of them and he described this period as "Standing by, Standing to, Standing down". The period of operational inactivity was a period in which Gibson met Eve Moore, at a party in Coventry, a city Gibson had gone to in order to visit his brother.

Evelyn Mary Moore was in Coventry as a dancer with the revue "Come out to Play" which was having its provincial premiere there at Coventry's New Hippodrome. The daughter of Ernest Edward Moore and Edith, nee Cole, who were in shipping at Penarth in Glamorgan, Eve was some seven years older than Guy but he summed her up as someone "who could discuss books, music and places. Most people who discuss these things well don't look so good, but this girl really was attractive".

Back at Scampton the weather was proving an obstacle. The Squadron ORB records the grim tale: "Feb 1st –13th No flying possible, weather

HANDLEY PAGE HAMPDEN
Guy Gibson went to war in the Handley Page
Hampden, the newest and most modern bomber in
the RAF in 1939. The crew accommodation was
notoriously cramped, so the Hampden came to be
nicknamed The Flying Suitcase by airmen.

13

HAMPDEN AND MINE, 1940
The Hampden was the only
RAF bomber able to carry naval
mines. Gibson was one of many
Hampden pilots sent out to drop
mines into German shipping
lanes - missions known in the
RAF as "gardening".

conditions prevailing during this period made operational work flying impossible aerodrome unserviceable owing to ice and snow." So it was perhaps a relief when the squadron transferred to Lossiemouth for anti-naval activities. Gibson himself arranged matters so his aircraft was flown up meaning he could take a train ride to Scotland because Eve was appearing in her show at Glasgow at that time.

Gibson describes the activities in this period as if on an idyllic holiday "Sometimes we would do a little flying," adding "I have never seen so much sea in my life with so little in it". The 29th February 1940, however, was to be a day when perhaps the squadron wished it had remained an empty sea. The No.83 Squadron ORB contents itself with the observation on 29th February: "8 aircraft carried out sweep. 1 aircraft dropped bombs on an unidentified submarine, result unknown, following officers and pilots took part S/Ldr Threapleton, F/O Mulligan, F/O Johnson, F/O Ross. F/O Gibson, Sgt Jenkins, Sgt Ollason". There was more to tell however, not least the fact that astute readers will have spotted that the numbers do not match (Sgt Sewell was also on the mission and was flying L.4057). Rather more unfortunate was the fact that the submarine was British.

Receiving orders to do a sweep in a 20-mile radius, eight Hampdens took off around 11.20. S/Ldr Threapleton's aircraft spotted a submarine, and opening his bomb doors dived on it. Later Threapleton was to state he was merely doing a full practice with the opportunity presented to him. However Sgt Ollason, who had also spotted the submarine, thought Threapleton had failed to drop his bombs because of his approach angle and therefore decided to attack the submarine himself. Ollason dropped his bombs, missing by 150 feet. Sgt Jenkins then fused his bombs but did not drop them, commenting

14

afterwards that he felt his attack position to be unsatisfactory. Between eight and ten minutes later, Jenkins spotted another submarine. "Receiving no recognition signal I assumed it was an enemy craft, and not having any orders to the contrary I decided to attack and dropped two 'B' bombs at the target." Harris, still in charge of 5 Group, later pointed out in the investigation, that this second submarine was indeed German.

Although Gibson said, "it was an unfortunate affair and was really no-one's fault but in the squadron records it is still written as a black mark" the RAF and Admiralty were less forgiving. The later Investigation Report concluded, inter alia, a failure to brief properly, poor W/T (Wireless Transmission) communications and protocols were to blame. The RAF response would be to impose tighter control over its men in the air. No.83 Squadron had meanwhile returned to Scampton on 19th March 1940.

Bomber Command strategy neither inclined them to, nor were they especially capable of, heavy attacks. In part this was because of the limited range and payload of British bombers, in part because the war was still being fought overtly and primarily against military targets. Therefore Gibson laid mines, attacked railways, bombed oil refineries and other targets. He wrote "These early raids were haphazard; we could choose our own route; we could bomb from any old height; sometimes we could carry whatever load we wished; we could go off at any time. We were individuals, but to tell the honest truth we were not very efficient."

Then, on 9 April 1940, Germany suddenly launched unprovoked invasions of Denmark and Norway. Denmark surrendered after just six hours, but Norway fought on. Gibson was among those sent up to drop mines in the areas being used by German invasion ships attacking Norway. Because the code names for the seaways were those of flowers or vegetables it was, perhaps, inevitable that sowing mines was called "gardening". In an eight-hour flight, on 11th April 1940, Gibson flew on a mission where mines were laid in the Great Belt (one of the three straits of Denmark that connect the North Sea and the Baltic), flying on to do a reconnaissance of Kiel Harbour to check on shipping, then to Middelfart in occupied Denmark to check on railway movements. Two days later the squadron received news that, in the Great Belt area troop ships had sunk.

On 14th April, Gibson flew, in appalling weather, back to Middelfart. Flying low, in the rain, Gibson headed towards the target before steadily dropping through the clouds. There is a pilot's phrase "fluffy clouds have hard centres", in this case they had wet ones. Gibson almost hit the sea, and hastily levelling out he saw the Middelfart Bridge looming up ahead of him. He flew straight underneath the central arch only to be fired on by a flak ship. Gibson recorded that his Hampden's bottom rear gunner returned fire as Gibson dropped his mines, then headed for cloud cover. Facing strong head winds, Gibson took two hours to reach Holland, then two more hours passed before he touched down at Manston in Kent.

A few missions in support of the British troops fighting in Norway followed, mine-laying in the Oslo Fjord and Kiel Canal before Gibson did his first attack on a German land target. On 10 May the main German assault in the West smashed into France, Belgium and Holland. The Allied armies were reeling back in some confusion and although the true magnitude of the German success had not yet become clear to the Allied High Command, it was felt that a major air offensive aimed at targets in Germany was warranted. On 17th May 1940 Gibson took off to bomb an oil refinery at Hamburg, one of 130 aircraft attacking German targets that night. Arriving when there was already a glow from one burning oil tank Gibson later recalled that, on his first run, diving down under the most intense light-flak he had then seen, the stack of four 500lb bombs did not release. Straining for every ounce of engine-power Gibson regained height to 5,000 feet in order to attempt a second run. By then, however, smoke was obscuring the oil refinery.

When eventually they were able to spot the target Gibson dived at a much steeper angle, with the Hampden reaching 320 mph. He released his bombs accurately, but the effort required to pull out from the dive was too much for Gibson, despite having both feet on the instrument panel. A hurried application of the tail-trim tabs produced the desired result. Shooting out at 2,000 feet over Hamburg, Gibson became an obvious target for flak, and a searchlight locked on to him. Gibson opened fire and soon despatched the searchlight. However, in the reflected light of the burning oil refinery, and mistaking a large piece of metal flapping on the wing for a fire, Gibson pressed the emergency signal to "abandon aircraft". Luckily for him the signal did not work and so gave Gibson time recognise his mistake. England definitely called ever more pressingly. Typically England was under fog when they arrived and after failing to put down at Scampton, Gibson landed at Abingdon in Berkshire.

Gibson
DFC

G ibson's next raid was also the RAF's second '100 bomber plus' raid, on the night of 21st/22nd May 1940. By this date the French front had been smashed wide open by the Germans at Sedan and panzers were surging west along the Somme Valley toward the Channel. The British Army in northern France and Belgium was in danger of being cut off from the rest of France. In an attempt to assist the French army, 124 aircraft were sent to attack railways and related transport targets. Gibson was one of six from No.83 Squadron, sent to attack the railway bridge over the Schelde-Maas canal, which mission he successfully completed hitting it directly with two 250lb bombs before landing at Mildenhall in Suffolk.

On 25th May, Gibson successfully dropped delayed action bombs into a railway tunnel near Aachen from a very low height. Flying along over the railway lines below tree-level Gibson and his crew finally spotted the cliff

GUY GIBSON
A portrait photo of Guy Gibson in RAF uniform. Gibson was a noted pipe smoker who often trailed the scent of his favoured blend of pungent tobacco in his wake.

looming up before them and pulling the stick back began a steep climb. Releasing two bombs at the commencement of the climb, Gibson avoided the cliff-face and the bombs exploded inside the tunnel precipitating a collapse. With two bombs left Gibson flew to the next tunnel on the map, about ten miles further on, only to discover that his second reconnaissance flare would not release itself. Co-pilot P/O Watson held an Aldis lamp

HAMPDEN AND CREWS
The crews of two Hampdens pose in front of one of the bombers for a formal RAF press photo issued in 1939. At this date more than 220 Hampdens were in service with eight squadrons in the RAF. It would be phased out of operational service by 1942.

shining forward to act as a spotlight. At 200 miles an hour the crew pressed on with this extempore arrangement and again released the two bombs as they began the climb. Clearing the 400-foot chalk face of the hill by a few feet the crew again blocked the entrance, and turned for home thankful no enemy fighters had been around.

On 26th May Gibson again attacked railway targets behind the German lines, then on 30th May he went back to Hamburg and on 9th June he was "gardening" again. There then came two of the few times in his career Gibson would not find the target. Failure to locate Givet, on the Franco-Belgian border, led to the bombing of Flushing (Vlissingen) aerodrome in south-west Holland instead; followed, in turn, by the failure to locate Hirson in Northern France and bombing a road junction.

Gibson's flight log-book for this period is missing, but he copied one entry into his memoir as: "June 13, 1940 - Hampden L.4070 - Pilot: self and crew - duty: bombing Ghent and England (nearly) - time: 7.5 hours". Gibson had bombed Ghent and was returning home under cover of darkness when caught by heavy searchlight/gun concentrations in low cloud. Gibson thought they were over Dunkirk, so flew due west looking for the French coast. Daylight came and Gibson's crew had not found the French coast. Spotting an aerodrome, and still having a bomb left, Gibson went into the attack, but pulled out when he recognised the airfield as RAF Harwell in the distinctly English Royal County of Berkshire!

By this date the evacuation of the British army from Dunkirk was over and the German panzer spearheads were driving deep into France. Paris fell on 14th June and France surrendered on 25th June. The collapse of France meant Britain now stood alone against the Nazi hordes. The only striking force that could readily make contact with Germany was the RAF. As part of the RAF strike force, and beginning to show his leadership qualities, Gibson was promoted to be a Flying Officer the announcement appearing in "The London Gazette" on 16th June 1939.

Gibson continued to attack specific targets, rather than area mine-laying, throughout June. The first week of July 1940 saw Gibson take part in the RAF switch to increased attacks on shipping. Key targets were the battlecruiser Scharnhorst at Kiel and the battleship Tirpitz, still under construction at Bauhafen Basin. It was during the attack on the Scharnhorst that Gibson dropped the first 2,000lb bomb of the war, during the night of

1st/2nd July. Gibson determinedly made six shallow dives from 6,000 feet but an unexpected three-second delay in the bomb release mechanism meant the bomb over-shot and landed in the town. Nevertheless, the RAF did hit the Scharnhorst on that raid.

On 9th July it was announced that Gibson had been awarded the Distinguished Flying Cross (DFC). The citation read, "In the course of eleven long-range operational flights, mostly at night, including raids on enemy plants and lines of communication, this officer has shown outstanding ability and devotion to duty. During one attack his aircraft hit an enemy balloon cable which cut through to the main spar of his starboard wing and then broke away. On the night of the 23rd May, 1940, he obtained two direct hits on a bridge over the Maas Canal; two nights later he successfully dropped delayed action bombs into a railway tunnel from a very low height. Flying Officer Gibson has at all times set an outstanding example to other pilots in his squadron by his enthusiasm, resourcefulness and courage."

Three more raids in July took Gibson to a leave which he spent in Cornwall with Eve. Returning to his squadron in August Gibson found many of his colleagues were no longer there and he was scheduled for operations. Gibson reveals attacking one E-boat and shooting up a Dornier 17 that very day – earning a 'probable' from Bomber Command.

Weather contributed to a failure unusual for Gibson throughout his career when he undertook to be on a solo mission from his squadron to attack the battlecruisers Gneisenau and Scharnhorst on 28th August 1940, with the battleship Bismarck as his secondary target. Gibson reported 9/10 cloud at 2,000 feet above Gneisenau and Scharnhorst with 10/10 cloud at 6,000 feet over Bismarck, and he returned with his bombs.

Early September saw four more raids – including the only time Gibson ever failed to complete a mission through technical problems when he returned, on 11th September 1940, with engine troubles. More happily, Gibson earned promotion to Flight Lieutenant on 3rd September, the promotion promulgated in "The London Gazette" of 19th November.

By this date the Battle of Britain had begun. As Fighter Command was heroically holding the line against German airborne attacks as part of Hitler's invasion plans, so Bomber Command attacked the barges that the Germans intended to use to carry their men and panzers across the Channel. The tactics of Bomber Command meant, basically, each bomber squadron had a specific port to attack, and each aircraft assigned an area within it. On 15th September 1940, Gibson's target was a basin in Antwerp harbour. The British did not know it but it was on this day that the German High Command postponed plans for the invasion of Britain. In the event the invasion never took place.

During another raid to the Channel ports, on 20th September, Gibson's aircraft was hit by flak just after a successful bombing run. One piece of lethal shrapnel missed Gibson's boot by half an inch, then tore off the toe-strap on the rudder bar. The rudder bar span forward, striking F/Sgt Houghton on the head and rendering him unconscious. The aircraft was otherwise undamaged, and Houghton soon recovered.

DORNIER DO17
Gibson became one of the few RAF bomber pilots to be credited with a "probable" air victory when he and his Hampden crew attacked a Dornier Do17, one of the fastest and most numerous bombers in the Luftwaffe at the time.

The next raid on 23rd September was a new Bomber Command record and Gibson's last operation with No.83 Squadron. For the first time over 200 aircraft, 209, were airborne on one night, and uniquely, at this point in the war, the main bombing strength, 129 aircraft, was sent to one city - Berlin. The Operational Orders for the night advised: "The moon will be two hours old over the target area at 23:45. The concentration of effort tonight is planned in retaliation of indiscriminate attacks in London. It is reported that the civilian morale has been greatly affected by our bombing". The raid was not wholly successful. With poor weather all the way to Berlin crews had to navigate by dead-reckoning. Although parts of Berlin were hit, bombing was scattered and largely ineffective.

Gibson was now at the end of his tour of duty. With Oscar Bridgeman having been shot-down and becoming a P.O.W. in Germany, Gibson was the last one left in the squadron from the beginning of the war, and he recorded a degree of melancholy when he went to bed that night. By surviving a full tour Gibson had earned a rest from operational duties, and the RAF expected Gibson to pass on his experience to others.

The RAF ran a number of Operational Training Units (O.T.U.) to prepare new crews for the realities of combat flying. One such unit was No.14 O.T.U. based at Cottesmore, and Gibson was to go there for his next base.

The unit ORB records on 26th September "F/Os Gibson, Withers and Murray and P/Os Lewis, Pinchbeck, Smith, Redpath and Mills reported on posting from Scampton and Waddington - exchange of operational areas". There is no more mention of him until 10th October, "F/O Gibson posted to 16 O.T.U. Upper Heyford". With an elegant symmetry the ORB for Upper Heyford records, on 10th October 1940, F/O G.P. Gibson (Pilot) arrived from No.83 Squadron for flying duties".

No.16 O.T.U. was tasked with training night bomber crews, for which the unit was equipped with Hampdens and Herefords (a variant of the Hampden with uprated engines). Gibson's log book for his time with No.16 O.T.U. has not survived, but he would have spent a lot of time in the air with new crews. The final entry for Gibson in the ORB records "26.11.1940 Flying Officer G.P. Gibson. (Pilot) of the screened staff was posted to 58 O.T.U. for flying duties". In fact by this date he had been flying for a fortnight with 29 Squadron in Fighter Command!

Into
Fighters

G ibson himself recalled, "...one day in October I received a blunt telegram from the Air Ministry:' Report to 29 (F) Squadron Digby for Flight-Command (Flying) Duties. Forthwith." The ORB for Digby records on 13th November, "...F/Lt G.P. Gibson arrived from Hexford on posting to 29 Squadron ..."and, predictably, Gibson's first entry in his No.2 (and only extant) Flying Log has him swiftly up in the air flying, on the 15th, doing an Ammunitions and Explosives (A/E) test.

BRISTOL BEAUFIGHTER
Gibson spent most of his time with RAF Fighter Command flying Beafighters. The long range and capacious fuselage of this aircraft made it ideal for service as a radar-equipped nightfighter. It was the main RAF nightfighter for two years from the autumn of 1941.

RAF Digby is near Scopwick in Lincolnshire, just over 11 miles from Lincoln. No.29 Squadron, at the time of Gibson's posting, had been flying Bristol Blenheims, but was now re-equipping with the Bristol Beaufighter. The Beaufighter first flew on 17th July 1939, entering service with the RAF on 2nd April 1940. Powered by two Hercules XI engines, developing a maximum speed of 335 mph, the Beaufighter was a potent weapon. With a service ceiling of 27,000 feet and armed with six Browning machine-guns firing .303 ammunition as well as four 20mm cannons, and an AI (Airborne Interceptor, a radar detection system) system the Beaufighter was well suited as a night-fighter. When No.29 Squadron completed transfer to the Beaufighter Mk IF it meant the beginning of squadron operations by a technically competent night fighter.

As a Flight Lieutenant in Fighter Command, Gibson was a Flight Commander – something that in Bomber Command would have required him to have the rank of Squadron Leader. Entering the Mess at The Grange, Wellingore, Gibson records he did not feel heartily welcomed. Over and above his feeling that, as a "bomber boy" he felt he was alien to the others, Gibson later wrote that the morale in the squadron was seriously defective. Old hands had been flying regular operations and not shot anything down, so, inter alia, the squadron seemed over-looked for commendations, and Gibson himself was replacing a highly popular acting Flight Commander.

Nevertheless Gibson's life was definitely changing. Gibson had recently become engaged to Eve. Guy and Eve had also acquired their own dog – a black Labrador named "Nigger". Nigger was allegedly a handful. One of Gibson's colleagues called him 'the black bastard', and others regarded him as a pest. Gibson, however, loved the dog and recalled him as "A great flyer was Nigger; he used to go up on nearly every patrol. I think it made him thirsty and he liked beer."

Gibson's first patrol was 19th November 1940, when he flew a Blenheim on an uneventful operation. On 22nd November Gibson recorded in his Flight log "To Cardiff (To be married!)". Gibson and Eve were married at All Saints Church, Penarth, in Glamorgan on 23rd November 1940. A honeymoon followed before Gibson returned, with Eve, to Lincolnshire, putting up at The Lion and Royal having been unable to find a house. At this stage, being in Fighter Command, Gibson was able to live with his wife but he did later comment it seemed hard on her sitting around waiting.

24

Gibson was back in the air, testing himself on the new Beaufighter. His first actual Beaufighter operation was on 10th December when he chased an on-board radar "blip" for fifteen minutes until it was identified as friendly by the controller on the ground. The following day saw action when, during a morning patrol, Gibson chased a Junkers Ju88 over the sea at about 1,500 feet some 60 miles east of Mablethorpe. Firing two short bursts at approximately 800 yards range Gibson chased the German into cloud. Because Gibson saw no damage he made no claim – it was a characteristic of Gibson's debriefs that he did not give consciously over-creative accounts of his activities.

Three uneventful patrols followed, then on 21st December Gibson witnessed a Junkers Ju88 shot down by light AA guns near Manby. Later that night Gibson spotted an enemy aircraft caught in searchlights over Horncastle. Gibson at once began to stalk the intruder, but was unable to close before it escaped into the dark. Uneventful patrols followed, the weather at the beginning of 1941 being so bad Gibson recalled that the squadron flew only one night sortie in the whole of January.

It was not until 4th February 1941 that Gibson was next in combat. Gibson generally now flew with Sergeant James and together on this night they started a patrol at 18:35. Patrolling at 10,000 feet, Gibson received vectoring directions from base to go to the Mablethorpe area, making an AI blip at 19:08 when investigating a flare. Spotting an aeroplane in searchlights, at 19:19, Gibson went over to investigate but discovered it was another Beaufighter. Patrolling between Grimsby and Spurn Head between 7,000 and 9,000 feet, Gibson followed a line of flares and, at 19:55, spotted an enemy aircraft - illuminated by the flares it had dropped. Gibson closed to 500 yards before firing a three-second burst but contact was lost in the night sky when the flares went out.

However, James had re-established an AI contact and Gibson followed it, but contact was again lost in manoeuvres. The German aircraft dropped another line of flares, each flare burning brightly for about 15 seconds dropping 1,000 feet behind the enemy aircraft in multiples of six. Following similar tactics as he had earlier, Gibson approached and saw the same, or a similar, aircraft in stark reality at 20:05; Gibson closing to 200 yards before giving another three-second burst. On neither occasion was return fire received nor any result of firing noticed. Because of this action, Gibson made his first entry in the Squadron ORB since his arrival. It is perhaps worthy of comment that, outside Hollywood, whilst an aircraft may be hit it does not necessarily crash, or indeed may do so later on; equally Gibson's C/O, Charles Widdows, shot a Junkers Ju88 down with 22 rounds. Gibson himself was to comment of his air-firing "...though I wasn't good, I was not completely bad".

It was during this period that Gibson records the improvements in the Airborne Interception device. AI relied on teamwork between the pilot and the observer, with the latter operating the instruments that helped locate other aircraft. There was also a strong interface with the Operations Room who, unlike in Bomber Command, could usually see the bigger picture because fighter operations involved aircraft solely flying over England or local waters.

RAF DIGBY OPS ROOM
The Sector Operations Room at RAF Digby, Lincolnshire, has been preserved as it was in 1939. It would not have looked very different when Gibson served here in 1940.

Nevertheless, the sky is a big place, there were eleven uneventful patrols before, on 13th March 1941, Gibson, and James obtained a "blip" four miles southwest of Sutton Bridge. The German had been dropping incendiaries near Grantham and was escaping at low altitude flying from cloud to cloud. Gibson fired from 800 yards before contact was broken. After landing, Gibson saw the radio plots that revealed the bomber had taken a wide circle and disappeared at the point that Gibson fired. As Gibson commented later of this combat "Naturally we did not claim anything because no one could honestly say that it had been destroyed, or even damaged." This punctiliousness is much to Gibson's credit – it is not precise what constitutes an "ace" – though the term as originally used in World War I meant a pilot who had shot down five enemy aircraft in combat. Whatever measure is used, Gibson may have attained Fighter Ace status if he had been less reticent about claiming kills.

The following day, on 14th March over Skegness, Gibson and James again made contact and engaged in combat. A Heinkel He111 seen flying at 13,000 feet off the Humber mouth ensured Gibson adopted the sound hunting technique of approaching the German, silhouetted against the stars, from the darkness of the land. Squarely in his sights, Gibson pressed the trigger – to a resounding silence! The Beaufighter, at this time, had no heated cockpit so frozen armaments were a frustratingly common problem. Indeed, only the day before, F/O Braham had had the same problem in combat. Following the German for fifteen minutes, while James worked to clear the guns, Gibson, with steady determination, closed again and this time a cannon worked. Gibson, believing from the absence of return fire that he had killed the rear gunner, closed for a third time and again nothing fired. James was working on the guns trying to free them as the German dived for the sea and a run to the Fatherland.

Gibson's task was to continue the contact – neither James nor any other Observer could simultaneously fix guns and work AI – and James was busy freeing a cannon. Gibson decided to aim for the port engine, a shrewd move designed to reduce the ability of the German to escape. Gibson was right on target and sparks flew as the Heinkel lost its engine. A few seconds later and the same treatment hit the starboard engine. The Heinkel headed to earth, and Gibson saw a man jump. Then a piece broke off the German aircraft and damaged the Beaufighter's wing. Gibson and James had the satisfaction of watching the German aircraft go into the sea off Skegness Pier. The whole

27

episode had lasted twenty minutes and the next day Gibson and James went to Skegness to collect the tail assembly as a squadron souvenir – Gibson recording his distaste for those who had looted a watch and an Iron Cross.

Because of the problems Gibson and James had encountered with their weapons, and many other incidents across the RAF, the Beaufighters were subsequently fitted with cockpit heating.

Gibson was involved in action of a very different kind when, after a patrol on 8th April, he came in to land at Wellingore: a Digby satellite station ten miles south of Lincoln. Gibson was flying with a Sergeant Bell, who was on a one-week attachment from 219 Squadron, and their patrol had started at 21:57. The patrol had been uneventful and, at 23:48, Gibson came in to land, not easy on Wellingore in a Beaufighter, which ideally preferred a longer runway. Gibson was on his landing approach, 50 feet above the ground, when a German Ju88, part of the raid designated x497, approached him from above and behind. Neither of the Beaufighter crew having seen him approach, the German strafed Gibson who was unable to return fire. Although Sergeant Bell received a leg wound from the German fire, Gibson was uninjured and managed to land the aircraft, despite going through a hedge in the process, with some minor damage to the brakes. German records suggest that the pilot of the German aircraft was Hans Hahn of 1./NJG 2.

Five miles south-east of Digby, on 17th April was when Gibson next made contact with the enemy, but the AI blip was lost

On 23rd April Gibson recorded in his log-book as "a great night". Recording ten blips and two visuals Gibson made visual contact on the second "blip", which was a Dornier 17. Gibson and James were east of Boston, flying at 10,000 feet and made contact at 01:06. Firing two short bursts Gibson believed he had damaged the Dornier but broke off contact in the face of extremely accurate return fire from the German's top rear turret.

Fighter Command decided to transfer 29 Squadron from No.12 Group into No.11 Group and base it at West Malling as part of the defence of London. Accordingly the C/O, Gibson, and another flew to West Malling to inspect the premises on 25th April 1941. The move happened across 28-30th April with "A" Flight recorded in the ORB as arriving on the 30th. Gibson's flight-log records on 29th setting off at 22:50 for a one and a quarter hour flight "From Wellingore to West Malling in formation of 8. Everyone very pleased to leave – including Fritz and Nigger!" This remark Gibson's

C/O, Charles Widdows owner of Nigger's companion Fritz, felt compelled to endorse "I agree". RAF Digby chose in their ORB to comment, on 1st May "29 Squadron did one night patrol in the early hours of the day and later left for WEST MALLING on posting"

West Malling was described by Gibson as "Of all the airfields in Great Britain, here, many say (including myself) we have the most pleasant." In Kent, near Maidstone, West Malling was a WWI landing area that became Maidstone Airport in 1932 before the military reclaimed it because of the increasing German militarism. Gibson's quarters were in the old Maidstone Flying Club Club-house, the Officer's Mess was a Victorian country house known as The Hermitage, the ground crew were in an old castle - and the local pub was "The Startled Saint".

HEINKEL HE111, 1940
The He111 was the mainstay of the Luftwaffe's bombing force for much of the war. This is an early model with a conventional cockpit, later variants had a fully glazed nose and smooth silhouette. More than 6,500 of these bombers were built by Germany.

Within their first three operations Gibson, and James, were both involved in a successful operation at their new base. The day started cloudy and cold, but by the evening the bright moon-light meant several patrols were undertaken. Gibson shot down an unidentified aircraft, as confirmed by the Observer Corps, following a successful vectoring from Biggin Hill.

On his next operation, 7th May, Gibson was again on night patrol when, according to his flight records, "X Raid – one destroyed by lucky burst. It blew up. Another did the same before I could open fire." This was however off-set by an infuriating and frustrating period between 10th and 19th May Gibson records with much frustration in both his book and his log-book.

On 10th May Gibson was part of an operation explicitly designed to protect London. Spotting two Heinkel He111s, Gibson closed in only to find his cannons would not fire. Undeterred Gibson made use of his Browning machine guns. Although recording damage to one Heinkel, again Gibson made no claim in the absence of tangible evidence of the destruction of the German aircraft. In fact, this was the beginning of tests on the 11th and two on 13th where the cannons would still not fire under tests. Testing his guns again, on the 19th, Gibson records in his flight-log. "Air firing again – NBG". Finally, on the 19th, after missing two certain Heinkel contacts and reduced operational opportunities thereafter, Gibson recorded the cannons all fired. Gibson revealed the problem in his memoirs – an electrical solenoid in the firing button – making an expensive fighter unserviceable!

DFC
Gibson won his Distinguished Flying Cross (DFC) in July 1941, being awarded the bar the following year. During the war 20,354 RAF officers were awarded the DFC, with 1,550 being awarded the bar. The horizontal bars of the cross are composed of wings, the upright bars are the blades of a propeller.

RAF WEST MALLING
Along with all RAF stations and squadrons, RAF West Malling was granted an heraldic badge in the 1930s. The badge features the nearby ruined castle and the motto "Portam Custodimus", "The Gate Keeper" a reference to both the castle and the role of the station as a fighter base protecting London.

The rest of the month, and indeed most of June, passed in fruitless patrols for Gibson. These were patrols with no sightings and sometimes not even a blip – save for 11th June with three blips, and 29th June with one visual contact but where the German successfully evaded action.

However this period saw some personal changes that affected Gibson. On 13th June 1941 the Squadron C/O, Wing Commander Widdows, took command of West Malling Station, and Wing Commander Colbeck-Welch became the squadron C/O. On 27th June S/Ldr Maxwell went to No 3 F.T.S. at South Cerny awaiting a posting to America or Canada. Two days later Gibson received promotion to Squadron Leader, and F/O Braham promotion to Flight Lieutenant. Strictly speaking Gibson was, at this period, an Acting Squadron leader such were the nuances of ranks awarded in the RAF around a matrix for Auxiliaries, Short Service, war-time Commissions, and permanent Officers, which this book is not intending to go into.

Gibson's first operation as a Squadron Leader was the day of his promotion. On 29th June, Gibson got two blips – despite no visual contact the best result in some time; however two more days of poor patrols followed, then double blips on 5th July before some real action.

On 6th July Gibson and James were on patrol during another raid on London. That night the Squadron shot down two Germans, whilst another squadron shot down a third - considering this was about twenty per cent of the number sent over, it was a "very good night" as Gibson later recorded. Gibson blew up a Heinkel He111 at 4,000 feet, firing a two-second burst that saw the German bomber burst into flames and crash into the sea, and Braham shot down a Junkers Ju88. By the end of July Gibson could confidently assert in his log-book, the official record agreeing, he had "three destroyed, one probable, and one damaged" to his credit.

However there then followed another long lean operational period for Gibson. For 24 operations, until 24th October 1941, Gibson patrolled, practiced searchlight co-operation and saw only one Heinkel and had a few blips – mainly he discovered the sky was vast and often empty, but the training was useful as it was when, on 9th August he returned on only one engine. The frustration was evident; against his monthly tally, Gibson bracketed them all and added "still" in September. The static nature of his tally did not stop Gibson gaining a Bar to his DFC, the papers confirmed with the Crown on 8th September and the Gazette publishing it on 16th September 1941. The London Gazette citation reads, "This officer continues to show the utmost courage and devotion to duty. Since joining his present Unit, Squadron Leader Gibson has destroyed three and damaged a fourth enemy aircraft. His skill was notably demonstrated when, one night in July, 1941, he intercepted and destroyed a Heinkel III." The papers sent to the King however had continued, "whilst flying at only 4,400 feet".

Gibson recorded damaging two Junker Ju87s, the "Stuka" dive bomber, when patrolling off Dover on 21st October, writing forlornly that, "a lonely watcher on the cliff said he saw one go into the sea but it was never confirmed", however that was very much his last hurrah in Fighter Command. Gibson's remaining patrols lacked combat action, a few blips and visuals but no action. In early November Gibson flew to Scampton, recording later that, on the 7th November visit, there were not many familiar faces. Visiting "Sunny Scampton", as duly recorded and called in his flight log-book, seems to have fed the lingering discontent with his role in fighters for Gibson records in his book it was so, also recording a new Bomber Command development – cameras.

With the exception of the "Battle of the Barges", feedback on bombing accuracy had not been especially accurate nor scientific, allocating bomb craters to individual aircraft on individual raids carried out on a few nights was not easy. However, "the boffins" had come up with a camera to take photographs from the bombing aircraft as the bombs fell. Gibson later recalled talking to someone called Ord who answered to the accuracy of the system, "To within a few hundred yards. When you press the tit a flashbomb goes off at the same time as the bombs; it explodes at about 3,000 feet and lights up the ground while the camera shutter is opened for just about the right time." Gibson records leaving convinced he should return to bombers. His frustration was later summed up by his remark that perhaps serves as a leitmotiv for why he flew, "flying is great fun if there is some point in it; if something's going to happen".

Although Gibson also recalled the squadron with affection and that he felt "Night flying was good fun and not too dangerous. There was absolutely no nerve strain, and I felt I could go on for ever" he was clearly unsettled but in the end, the RAF took a different view. The RAF decided Gibson needed a rest and they were going to transfer him to an O.T.U. forthwith. Gibson pointed out he had come to Fighters for a rest but what Bomber Command may say had no merit in the eyes of Fighter Command and on 24th December the Squadron ORB recorded "Squadron Leader Gibson left the station having been posted to Cranfield NF O.T.U.".

Gibson's official record at 29 Squadron was three shot down, one probable and three damaged. Had he been less punctilious it seems Gibson could have tried to claim for at least four shot down three probables and five damaged. Had Gibson been the glory-seeker the discontented allege it is probable he would have been less scrupulous in his claims – modesty and understatement of achievements are not typical for glory-seekers. However during his time in Fighter Command Gibson did advance – he gained a DFC (the RAF recognised his colleague on all successful operations, Sgt James, by awarding him the DFM), a Bar to his DFC, promotion to Squadron Leader and added broader skills to his experience by leading A Flight. Leaving the Squadron, Gibson's official rating was "above average" in both night-fighter flying and air gunnery, but despite this he realised he did indeed belong in Bomber Command for, as Gibson later put it in an interview in Canada, "I just joined really for fun".

An Interlude
of Training

I t is proverbial among servicemen that the RAF moves in predictable ways and, his ability in night-fighters confirmed by assessment, deed, and promotion, Gibson received a posting to an O.T.U. – the very thing he had joined Fighter Command to evade!

The RAF decided they required Gibson, as Chief Flying Instructor, in No.51 Operational Training Unit that was a Night Fighter unit. Because of this, with the logic beloved of the Armed Services, Gibson, who had been flying Beaufighters, went to an O.T.U. that used Blenheims and Havocs – and which was, at that time, based at Cranfield.

No.51 Unit formed on 26th July 1941 at Debden as part of No 61 (Training) Group within Fighter Command. Opened in 1937 in Bedfordshire, RAF Cranfield was between Bedford and Milton Keynes, and much of it is now the site of Cranfield University.

Gibson did not want to go, he freely admits to lobbying both Fighter Command and 5 Group HQ to avoid the posting, but to no avail. Gibson's old commander in 5 Group, Arthur Harris had moved on to other duties and had been replaced by Air Vice Marshal Norman Bottomley who did not know Gibson. Interestingly, five year later Bottomley would succeed Harris as head of Bomber Command, but that was a long way into the future.

The Cranfield ORB records, against 29th December 1941, "S/Ldr G.P. Gibson posted from 29 Squadron for C.F.I. duties". Gibson does not reappear in the ORB until he left on 23rd March 1942, when it recorded, "S/Ldr G.P. Gibson, CFI, posted to No.106 Squadron. S/Ldr A.T. Stavely assumed duties of CFI"

Whilst commenting, "I would never say I was not happy" and "life was not unpleasant" as well as describing the Unit as "a happy place where everyone saw the fun in life", Gibson did not speak much about the three months of his time at Cranfield. The ORB only mentions Gibson's arrival and departure and flight log-books do not always spell out the "why?" just the "what?".

RAF CRANFIELD
Seen from the air as it is today, Cranfield Airport is
a private airfield used for pilot schools. In 1941
RAF Cranfield was likewise a training base. Gibson
flew over 1,400 hours during his time here as he
trained new pilots in the skills needed for combat.

Gibson's log-book, records his disgruntlement graphically: "With the New Year I am posted as C.F.I. to 51. O.T.U. Cranfield, this being held as a rest from operations!!!" The log-book shows Gibson flew 1,406 hours thirty minutes that period, and shows a vast array of aircraft flown: Magister, Lysander, Dominie, Blenheim, Wellington, Tiger Moth, Cygnet, and Oxford. The "missions" amounted to training, taking up ATC cadets, going to parties, CFI tests, and trips to assorted airfields. However we do know that the ORB for Gibson's period at Cranfield records 4 Blenheims crashing, and 1 Boston; 5 people killed; 135 pupils in, 102 out; 139 hours and 20 minutes night-flying and 433 hours fifty minutes day-time flying. There must be speculation about how much of that total was Gibson's. However, it comes as no surprise that when an aircraft was sent up on a hazardous five minute flight to check if it was safe for others to fly, it was Gibson who piloted the aircraft.

On 16th December 1941, Gibson was Gazetted as a Temporary Squadron Leader, w.e.f. the 1st December. Gibson was still lobbying and by now the time and tide of affairs was running his way as, within the wider RAF, other changes were taking place.

After a spell as a senior staff officer, Arthur Harris was promoted to the rank of Air Marshal and became C-in-C Bomber Command in February 1942, and Gibson seized his chance. Harris was stepping up Bomber Command's offensive against Germany, and, at this stage of the war, that was indeed the only concerted offensive against Germany. Gibson says he saw the pictures of the attacks on the Renault works at Billancourt near Paris, whilst he was in the Cranfield Mess "and having had a hectic morning testing doubtful pilots in an old Blenheim with a sputtering port engine, I decided I would have to get back somehow to bombers".

Billancourt was the most significant raid of the war so far in many ways: 235 aircraft sent on the largest raid so far, with 121 bombers an hour pounding the target against a previous Bomber Command best of 80 an hour, meant Bomber Command was starting to deliver on the potential it had always proclaimed for itself. Bomber Command was attacking the enemy, Gibson wanted to be there. Gibson was summoned to an interview with the C-in-C on 12th March 1942 and two days two hours later was posted to command No.106 Squadron at Coningsby via a token appointment to 5 Group HQ on 23rd March 1942.

The Billancourt raid was a significant change in Britain's war policy. The War Cabinet had been reluctant to attack industrial targets in the German occupied countries but on 2nd February 1942 they had reversed that decision. Gibson had seen the photographs of the first effective and significant precision raid under Harris' leadership, a night when 235 bombers in good weather and perfect visibility demonstrated incontrovertibly what a strong bomber force could achieve. The other key change in strategy, and there is no knowledge if this influenced Gibson, was when the new policy of "area bombing" was authorised on 14th February wherein, "It has been decided that the primary objective of your operations should now be focussed on the morale of the enemy civil population and in particular of the industrial workers."

The tactic of area bombing was simple in concept, but was to prove to be difficult in practice. Reconnaissance photos had shown that the standard of bomb aiming by RAF bombers was fairly poor. Asked to hit a single factory, a small proportion of pilots could get a bomb on target, but a very much larger number could get a bomb within half a mile of the factory. The idea behind area bombing was that instead of specifying a single target – which might well be missed by every bomb – the RAF planners would instead designate an area of a square mile or more to be hit. Care was taken to locate areas of this size that contained a large number of factories, railway stations, canal junctions and other worthwhile targets. The bombers were then sent out with orders to hit the area, which they could be relied upon to do with a fair degree of accuracy, and so to damage or destroy the various targets within it.

Inevitably there would be within the designated area a large number of other things, and these would also be bombed and destroyed. Such collatoral damage might include roads, houses, offices, shops, churches and schools. Inevitably civilians would be killed. At the time that area bombing was devised, this was considered to be just about acceptable. The only places where enough worthwhile targets were grouped close enough together to be an area worth bombing were in industrial cities where weapons and war material were being produced. The civilians living there were certainly either making the weapons, or supporting those who did. In an age of total war such civilians were not deemed to be innocent, but to be part of the war effort of Hitler's Reich. Their destruction was never the target of the RAF, but if some of them were killed then nobody in the RAF was going to lose much sleep over the fact. After all the Germans had bombed Coventry, Rotterdam and Warsaw with a total disregard for civilian casualties.

There were other problems relating to navigation that sometimes saw RAF bombers arrive over a completely different town from the one they were supposed to bomb, but such navigational errors were unrelated to area bombing. They would have occurred even if the RAF had continued with its original policy of precision bombing.

Harris, who did not help conceive the concept of area bombing but knew that British bombers were sitting ducks during the day, and generally speaking lacked the ability to hit precision targets in the dark, found the order on his desk when he took over Bomber Command. He was to introduce reforms to tactics and equipment that made Bomber Command a ferociously effective instrument of war.

Harris already knew Gibson from his No.83 Squadron days when Harris had commanded 5 Group. Harris had then been in the habit of visiting the bases under his command, and given the task Harris faced in Bomber Command having the determined Gibson back in the fold made eminent sense. Harris had 48 squadrons at his disposal, of which 38 were actually operational, and a further five consisted of light-bombers wholly unsuitable for attacks on Germany. Of these 44 squadrons only fourteen had the new heavy bombers, the Halifax, Stirling, and Manchester, Bomber Command had no "big hitting" strike force. Harris knew he needed people such as Gibson to strike at Germany as required by the Air Staff and the War Cabinet. Harris had made clear that he thought Gibson a "firebrand" and that some of the other commanders in Bomber Command were not. So he hinted to Air Vice Marshall Slessor, Air Officer Commanding (AOC) 5 Group, that Gibson was ready for a command. Gibson in fact went on leave after his CFI duties, Eve had gone to Penarth after the West Malling tour ended ,where she was engaged in war work for the Red Cross in the POW section.

Most importantly, as Gibson later wrote "In a years' work, involving about seventy night sorties and thirty day patrols, I had in all seen about twenty Huns. Of these I had opened fire on nine. Obviously I was not a very good shot. And bombing was still in my blood."

First Squadron
Command

On 13th April 1942 Gibson was promoted to Acting Wing Commander from a substantive of Squadron Leader to make him eligible for command. In Bomber Command it was necessary to be a Wing Commander to command a Bomber Command squadron. Gibson then took his position as Commanding Officer of No.106 Squadron. Of command Gibson was later to write "I didn't do as much as the boys, but used to content myself with one trip every five nights. No Squadron-

AVRO MANCHESTER ON GROUND
The Manchester entered service full of promise, but Gibson was one of many pilots who soon came to curse the bomber's notoriously unreliable engines. Avro stopped production only a few months after the bomber entered service, switching their efforts to the infinitely better Lancaster.

106 SQUADRON CREST

No.106 Squadron was based near Doncaster at the time it was granted an heraldic badge, so it borrowed the lion rampant carrying a banner from that town's coat of arms, adding an astral crown and the motto "Pro Libertate", which translates as "For Freedom".

Commander can for that matter. [He must do] paperwork, write long-casualty letters and run the squadron generally, plan the next raid, organise the bomb and petrol loads, organise the crews". The future would prove that Gibson was to remain a more active flying C/O whenever the chance arose.

Formed in World War I, then disbanded until June 1938, No.106 Squadron had a largely training role within 5 Group until early 1941. Newly returned to front-line status, the Squadron was still flying Hampdens when they transferred to Coningsby in February 1941, but the squadron had converted from Hampdens to the Manchester heavy bomber earlier in 1942.

Coningsby's ORB records the station opened on 7th January 1941 and that No.106 Squadron was the first bomber squadron to occupy it. In March 1941, No.97 Squadron, operating Avro Manchesters, arrived at Coningsby. Developed in response to Air Ministry Specification in May 1936 which called for a twin engined bomber to be powered by the Rolls Royce Vulture engine, the Manchester was a very strong aircraft, having a very large single celled bomb bay taking up some two thirds of the fuselage length but it was also an aircraft with inherent engine problems. The twelve-cylinder Vulture was neither as powerful, nor as reliable, as expected by the time the first prototype flew in July 1939. The Manchester's maximum speed was 265mph at 17,000 feet, it could cruise at 185 mph at 15,000 feet, had a notional ceiling of 19,200 feet that was not always readily attainable and a range varying between 1630 miles with 8,100lb of bombs and 1200 miles with 10,350lb of bombs. The ill-fated Manchester would later be redesigned with the same fuselage, but extended wings able to house four Rolls Royce Merlin engines. The Manchester thus became the much-loved Avro Lancaster.

When 97 Squadron converted to the heavier, but much superior, Lancaster they had to leave for Waddington because they made Coningsby's grass runways too rutted. Gibson, the former Hampden pilot, arrived after the squadron did their last Hampden operation on 10th March 1942 and as they were re-equipping with Manchesters.

Gibson recalls he met some of his command at a dance in the WAAF's mess, then others more formally later. Impressed by their discipline about abstemious drinking before operations Gibson was less impressed by the lack of discipline when he first met the NCO aircrews who seemed, on that occasion, to have a more relaxed attitude towards King's Regulations. Not a naturally enthusiastic administrator within the office, Gibson found Bomber Command to be very paper-driven but records the Adjutant and he were lucky to have an excellent Orderly Room Corporal. However, Gibson felt that both the flight commanders had fatigue and he felt they needed replacing. Gibson replaced them both fairly speedily, though he did so with some sympathy.

As well as familiarising himself with the state of his command Gibson's log-book shows he put flying time in getting to know the Manchester. After F/Lt Robinson showed Gibson the ropes there were other cross-country exercises and more night flying training. Gibson's first operation was, in some ways, a throw-back to his days in No.83 Squadron as once again he laid mines in the Baltic on 22nd April 1942, but he needed operational experience in a Manchester. Throughout his tenure as C/O, Gibson always tried to send new crews on mine-laying operations as a gentle way to introduce them to wartime operations, clearly he applied it to himself as well.

Gibson's first 'enemy coast ahead' operation for No.106 Squadron was the medieval town of Rostock, a busy port with submarine building yards, and with the Heinkel works nearby at Marienhehe. The RAF attacked Rostock four nights in a row, 23rd-26th April, and not surprisingly some pilots questioned why they had not just had a large force in one night. Indeed the pilots were right and the Germans not being slow on the uptake had increased flak defences by the third night. Gibson, in an early demonstration of willingness to challenge Group HQ asked what underpinned the approach – but later wrote that nobody knew there either.

For the raid on 25 April, Gibson's squadron was given the task of hitting the main hangars of the Heinkel works. It was not unusual for Bomber Command to specify that a particular squadron – or sometimes even a single aircraft – should break away from the main bomber force engaged in an area attack in order to attack a specific, small target. The idea was that the squadron would gain all the defensive and navigational advantages of being part of the bomber force on the outward journey, but would then peel off to carry out an old-style precision attack of the type with which Gibson had been familiar when flying Hampdens. It also had the advantage of keeping the German defenders guessing. They would be unable to concentrate all their forces on the main force if they knew that some bombers would be likely to divert to attack a second target.

These orders to attack the Heinkel works resulted in another instance of Gibson's refusal to accept orders at face value. Group demanded that the raid be carried out from a height of over 4,000 feet so that the on-board cameras (by now becoming an operational sine qua non in Bomber Command) could record the results. But the target was relatively small and, in Gibson's view, could be hit reliably only from a height of 2,000 feet or so. Gibson questioned the order, but Group was insistent. He then ordered his pilots to go in at 2,000 feet anyway and ignore the need for photographs.

Actually out on the operation, Gibson opted for bombing from 3,500 feet. He hit the target, as did many others of his squadron, and pleased with the results flew back low. En-route the squadron flew over moored U–Boats whereupon Gibson circled over them until feeling he had gleaned sufficient information for naval intelligence. Goebbels recorded that 70% of houses in the city centre had been destroyed and, recording his lunchtime conversation with Hitler, makes the interesting observation, "He shares my opinion absolutely that cultural centres, health resorts and civilian centres must be attacked now" as if there had been no German raids on seaside resorts, or Bath, or other cities at that point!

The following night saw Rostock attacked again, a raid not undertaken by Gibson, and it was in reporting these four days of raids that Goebbels publicly used the phrase 'terror raid' for the first time - conveniently forgetting the

London Blitz et al! More significant than the fulminations of the Reich's Minister for Propaganda was his own acknowledgement that "there was in fact panic" and "more than 100,000 people had to be evacuated" and "community life there is almost at an end". Goebbels also commented, in terms Harris would have valued, that there was a real risk, "the workers' morale would be crushed flat by the bombing".

LANCASTERS ENTER SERVICE, 1942
The mighty Avro Lancaster bomber entered service with the RAF in 1942 and served to the end of the war. In that time it flew 156,000 sorties and dropped 619,000 tons of bombs. It also dropped food parcels into occupied Holland in early 1945, with permission from the Germans.

The night of 4th May 1942 saw Gibson engaged in a routine mine-laying operation off Sylt, little more than a team-building exercise for flight crew, as far as his involvement went, although clearly having an important role in keeping German shipping less than free to roam the seas.

Gibson's next raid was again on Heinkel works but this time at the Warnemunde factory, a few miles along the coast from Rostock, where he was part of an attacking force of 193 aircraft. Gibson attacked from 3,500 feet encountering fierce opposition in a raid Bomber Command called 'only moderately successful'.

In the spring of 1942, No.106 Squadron started to replace its problem-prone Manchesters with Lancasters. The Lancaster's first actual operation being on 19th May 1942, but Gibson only had time for one flight before falling ill and entering RAF Rauceby hospital for two weeks. Declared in need of a fortnight's sick leave, Gibson was flown to Cardiff, met his wife, and they holidayed inter alia at Portmeirion.

As a result Gibson, usually keen to engage in new forms of striking at the enemy, missed two Bomber Command innovations – streaming and The Thousand Bomber Raid. Streaming was a technique designed to overwhelm the opposition by sheer weight of numbers flying the same route at the same speed and height within a specified time slot. The Thousand Bomber Raids were designed to wipe out a target with one blow, but problems with bomb aiming meant they were less effective than hoped. They did, however, make for powerful propaganda here and abroad. In the event only three such raids were staged – the organisational strain of getting 1,000 bombers operational at the same time proved too much for Bomber Command to maintain.

Collected from Llanbedr at the end of June, Gibson started logging flying time and putting together a crew to ensure he was competent enough on Lancasters to go out on a sortie to Wilhelmshaven, with 284 other aircraft, on 8th/9th July 1942.

Although recording the operation as 'good going' in his log-book Gibson was, on reflection, less convinced as he later expressed doubts about the Standard Operating Procedure (SOP) and what he considered to have been a needless loss of life. Gibson knew crews had all been briefed that the target was lightly defended so all aircraft had been ordered to attack at low level. The target was easily located, the weather very clear and visibility good, but pilots discovered heavy flak they regarded as accurate and intense, augmented by the Germans laying searchlights horizontally across the target. Gibson and three others from his squadron felt they had hit the target, but records show most of the bombing fell in open country west of Wilhelmshaven.

The arrival of the 'heavy bombers' increased the strike options and range open to Bomber Command. Because of the RAF's enhanced strike capacity Bomber Command conceived an ambitious raid involving flying the 1,500 miles round trip to Danzig and attacking the submarine works located there.

The Danzig raid was a job for Lancasters, it was untried and it called for leadership so Gibson typically led by example contributing nine aircraft to the 44 scheduled to attack on 11th July 1942. The plan was for the Lancasters to fly in formation over the North Sea, utilise the expected cloud cover over Denmark and the Baltic and, with clear weather expected over Danzig, bomb from normal height as dusk fell and then make their way back to England under cover of night. In fact, weather conditions worsened, with cloud at sea level at the Danish Coast so aircraft pressed on as conditions allowed. Gibson was one of those who arrived too late to attack the target so diverted to the secondary target of Gdynia and attacking a ship with 5x1,000 lb bombs. Gibson reported that he missed by 20 yards from an altitude of 1,000 feet, and that they machine-gunned a flak ship on the way home.

Opposition over Danzig was not heavy, only two aircraft were lost whilst 24 aircraft bombed Danzig and returned. It was a good plan and certainly a triumph of long-range flying. However, with a third of bombers unable to locate Danzig, and the rest arriving late, it was clear that navigation over water was still a concern for Bomber Command. Gibson records 10-15 hours flying, Shannon recalled they both swapped places frequently to avoid cramp, and the R.A.F judged the technique of partial day flying a success. Two Sergeants from No.106 Squadron received DFMs for the raid.

A week later, on 18th July, Gibson took off for Essen, a heavily defended target in the Ruhr which, because of rain and low cloud in England, was felt to be worthy of some daylight operation. However, with the weather clearing over Europe, it meant the bombers would be fully visible to German fighters; all bombers received recall messages, Gibson himself receiving the message over Flushing and reversing course, jettisoned his bombs in the sea. Essen, indeed the Ruhr in general, was a hot-spot not relished by any but the most foolish in Bomber Command. Gibson however showed leadership means

SYLT HAMPDEN CREWS AFTER RAID, 1940
Gibson took part in the RAF raid on the German
seaplane base on the island of Sylt, off the North
Sea coast of Germany. Compared to later raids it
was small in scale, but the RAF made great
propaganda use of it, using photos such as this.

not just picking the easy enemy targets, and that heroism is as much about
overcoming fear as not being aware of it.

The Secretary of State for Air, Sir Archibald Sinclair, was not averse to
getting away from Westminster and seeing the RAF on the ground. Gibson
records in his log-book giving Sinclair, two Air Commodores and a Group
Captain a flight from Horsham St Faith, in Norfolk, to Coningsby in his
Lancaster with the words "I brought these gentlemen to see a crack
squadron". There is little doubt that No.106 Squadron, under Gibson,
certainly had the eye of Group HQ and Bomber Command itself. What the
log-book does not record is how there was nearly a military coup!

Gibson was flying with a new Flight Engineer and that, not unusually for
a politician, Sinclair wanted to see how things worked so encouraged Gibson
to feather an engine. Sinclair seemed pleased with the results so Gibson

feathered another engine, and a pleased politician wandered off to see how the rear turret worked. One of the senior officers then instructed Gibson after a few minutes of flying like this that they were in a hurry. Passing the order to unfeather the engines Gibson looked on with dismay as the Flight Engineer pressed the wrong buttons! Fortunately the Merlin was a reliable engine-plant and started swiftly, the flight proceeding with no further incidents.

Unlike Essen there was to be no recall when Gibson joined a maximum regular Bomber Command effort for Hamburg on 26th July when 403 aircraft formed the attack. Arriving in excellent visibility and easily locating the target in the moonlight, Gibson's Lancaster delivered its 9,500lb bomb load despite the inevitable heavy and accurate flak. The attacking force lost 7.2% of the aircraft, Gibson recording his aircraft nearly bought it coming out of Brunnsbattels - but his Flight Commander, who had checked him out on the Manchesters, F.H. Robertson, was the sole No.106 Squadron casualty that night.

The raid was a success even if, with a lot of the bombing being directed at existing fires, much of the bombing was SW of the aiming point. This phenomenon by which aircraft arriving later in a raid aimed at burning fires, and usually bombed short of those fires, rather than at the actual aiming point was to become known as "bombing creep".

German records show that at least 800 fires began, 523 classed as large, and the Hamburg fire department for the first time needed extensive reinforcement from other fire services. Estimates for compensation claims on this Hamburg raid were around 250 million Reichmarks or £25 million - at a time when a Lancaster cost around £43,000 depending on specification.

Gibson's final raid of July was a major one on Dusseldorf, amongst other things a city with the administrative departments of most Ruhr and Rhineland iron, steel, heavy-engineering, and armament companies. On 31st July Bomber Command, whilst consciously not attempting the 1,000 figure, still put up 630 aircraft and included some from training units. Gibson and 20 others took part with 18 aircraft of these hitting the target, one an alternative target, and one aircraft went missing - contributing to the 4.6 % of losses for Bomber Command. It was the first raid with over 100 Lancasters, and Gibson's was one that hit the target. Bombing from 12,000 feet, Gibson contributed to a squadron record of 63 tons of bombs dropped on a target - the squadron's contribution to more than 900 tons of bombs dropped that night.

The raid on Dusseldorf was a major success according to the incredibly detailed German records, which even include details of a cow udder injured by a bomb splinter! In Dusseldorf and its suburbs there were 453 buildings destroyed, 15,000 damaged, and 954 fires started.

July 1942 was the first full month Gibson had been in command of the Squadron, fully fit and with aircraft that were up to the tasks allotted. The results were as Harris would have wished, and justified his faith in Gibson. The squadron had set a new record for itself, and 5 Group, by dropping 293.7 tons of bombs, having made 84 operational sorties representing 359 flying hours - and as a result had raised their profile with national leaders. The increased activity saw five aircraft lost.

August began with uncharacteristic operations for Gibson, but he performed them with his typical determined and leadership style. Newcomers usually undertook mine-laying, or 'gardening', as a means of breaking them into operational flying, at lower risk than operations over mainland Europe. Such operations were usually carried out when the weather was good, but there was clearly an element of urgency when, in conditions of rain, mist 10/10 cloud at 500 feet that normally caused cancellations, No.106 Squadron was ordered into the Silverthorn and Forget-me-Not areas of the Baltic.

No.106 Squadron put up four crews of the 12 Bomber Command sent out. Gibson was one of two in Silverthorn and the squadron contributed two to the Forget-me-not area. Gibson successfully managed to drop four mines at 20-second intervals having finally located the point when they found the island of Skaw and made a timed run. This method of finding a target involved passing over a known landmark at a precise heading and speed, then determining distance flown by time taken and then dropping the bombs without seeing the target. In this instance it was used to hit a target of featureless sea, but could also be used over land if cloud obscured the actual target, but not a nearby landmark. On the gardening operation 75% of Gibson's squadron were successful, a testimony to the training and endurance - the C/O himself being airborne for seven hours and five minutes.

Two days later, on 10th August, with the squadron officially stood down from operations there was, in similarly poor weather, a call to arms for mine-laying again. Three scratch crews were hastily assembled, part of 52 called for by Bomber Command, again, the C/O showed his style of leadership by example and took part. Having made a dead-reckoning run off Helshov Point, Gibson successfully dropped his bombs and landed 7½ hours later.

The next scheduled operation over mainland Europe that Gibson undertook was on Mainz when 138 aircraft went for the second night in a row. Weather over the target was 10/10 cloud, there was considerable light flak, and this was the day, 12th August 1942, of the last large-scale attack on

CRASHED LANCASTER
The Lancaster bomber was to be the mainstay of RAF Bomber Command during the second half of the war. Although popular with crews, accidents did happen. This Lancaster crashed and caught fire when taking off from RAF Elsham Wolds in Lincolnshire.

Germany without Pathfinders. Gibson welcomed the pathfinder concept but, ironically, this raid on Mainz was one of the more successful raids - causing widespread damage to some 135 acres of the centre and industrial areas over the two nights. Gibson was the lowest bomber of his squadron at 6,000 feet - his colleagues bombing from 7, 9, 12, 16 and 17,000 feet. At one point flak and searchlights locked onto Gibson and he dived low to escape, again demonstrating his preference for low flying as a solution.

Pathfinder missions were to become the norm over Germany from 15th August 1942. The Pathfinder idea could be a source of friction between senior officers and the Pathfinder Commander "Pathfinder Bennett". Some officers resented their finest personnel being posted out from under them, some felt that the job was best done from within a squadron, some felt there was no need for a separate Group – and hostility was most marked at a senior

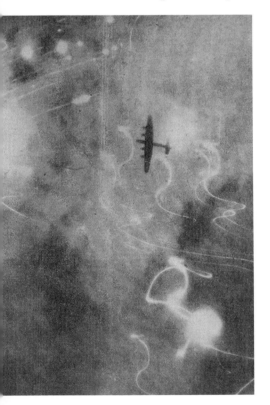

LANCASTER OVER HAMBURG
A Lancaster bomber is silhouetted against the light thrown up by the burning city of Hamburg in a photo taken from another RAF bomber. By 1942 bomber crews habitually dropped their bombs on marker flares dropped by pathfinder crews.

level in 5 Group. After his experiences at Wilhelmshaven, Gibson welcomed the idea of greater effectiveness in operations, and indeed by a twist of fate Gibson's old squadron, No.83, became the Pathfinder Squadron for 5 Group.

Under Guy Gibson No.106 Squadron had developed a reputation within 5 Group, so 106 had the special mission to attack the German aircraft carrier Graf Zeppelin by then at Gdynia along with the Gneisenau. The British had invented a new kind of bomb, the "capital ship bomb", a 5,500lb device with a shaped charge warhead designed to penetrate armour. Gibson, writing under the security strictures of the times described it as resembling a turnip with all the ballistic characteristics of one. With the bomb's poor ballistics there was a need for greater accuracy in the bomb sights and the Ministry of Aircraft Production produced a new bomb sight. With new bombs, new sights and repeated practice by 106, who soon could hit a target within 60 yards from 10,000 feet, the stage was set for Gibson's next operation.

On 27th August 1942, whilst 306 aircraft made a successful attack on Kassel, nine No.106 Squadron members made a special raid on Gdynia in the only Allied air attack ever specifically targeting Graf Zeppelin for attack. Gibson was flying with S/Ldr Richardson, from the Armament School at RAF Manby, not his usual bomb-aimer. Richardson had experience of the new sights and was heroically returning to operations having last been on active service in August 1918!

However weather again came to the German's aid as, after a 950 mile flight, 9/10 cloud and haze obscured visibility at Gdynia. With his trademark determination, Gibson flew over the target 12 times in an hour before bombing. Gibson again flew lowest at 8,500 feet, but missed by a hundred feet; it was Hopgood, bombing from 10,000 feet, who came closest to the Graf Zeppelin on this raid. One pilot was unable to see the carrier due to haze and instead dropped his bomb on the estimated position of the target.

Therefore, in the August of 1942, No.106 Squadron had flown on 15 nights: composed of 100 sorties and 523 operational hours flying time. Gibson flew four of these nights and contributed to new squadron records of bomb tonnage dropped (323) and 94 mines, with only three aircraft lost over the month.

Pathfinder operations were now normal over Germany but Gibson's first was on 1st September 1942. The raid showed that failures were still possible and that techniques still needed refining. Gibson was one of 11 from No.106

Squadron who made up a 231 aircraft striking force detailed to attack Saarbrucken in cloud-free, good visibility conditions. What should have been a success was, in fact, a technical success and an operational failure.

Some 205 aircraft claimed to have bombed the marked position - including Gibson and all of No.106 Squadron except Hopgood - and the photographs taken showed almost total obliteration. The next day the PRU (Photo Reconnaissance Unit) revealed the Pathfinders had dropped their markers on the non-industrial town of Saarlouis some 12 miles north of Saarbrucken. The mistake was thought to have been due to the fact that the bend in the Saar River at Saarlouis was of a similar shape to that at Saarbrucken. Hopgood had in fact bombed the correct target - it not being clear if this was a feat of superior navigation, or poor bomb-aiming.

Some two weeks later, on 13th September, Gibson flew one of 446 aircraft - his own squadron contributing 12 operational aircraft - that attacked Bremen, a heavily defended port city on the River Weser, close to the North Sea coast. The city was covered in haze, despite the otherwise good weather. Gibson bombed from 11,000 feet against a squadron average of 13,000 feet, again the lowest in the squadron. A bomb-aimer killed in another aircraft was the squadron's only loss, all of Gibson's aircraft returned despite losses of 4.7% for Bomber Command. Luck in part, but luck requires courting - thorough training with ability and willingness to argue with Group HQ by their Squadron Commander suggests No.106 Squadron were, if not defying the odds, at least bettering them.

The raid itself was a success. Bremen, notable for U-Boat construction yards, Lloyd dynamo and Focke-Wulf, was a target that Bomber Command then ignored for five months! This inaction despite the Lloyd dynamo works being out of action for two weeks; and parts of the Focke-Wulf factory out of action for two to eight days, as well as damaging three new aircraft and destroying four seems a contrary policy when the RAF attacked Rostock four days in a row.

On Gibson's next raid, Wismar on 23rd September, the Pathfinders were not present through bad weather but 83 Lancasters of 5 Group set out to attack this Baltic Coastal town and the nearby Dornier aircraft factory. Despite the weather, no pathfinders, and a 5% loss to Bomber Command the RAF successfully hit the target causing extensive damage. Gibson recorded in his log, "hit it ok with our incendiaries".

The approach of autumn brought rains, and this meant that No.106 Squadron started to face the problems 97 Squadron had experienced and so it finally became necessary to lay concrete runways at Coningsby. The decision to upgrade Coningsby meant No.106 Squadron transferred to Syerston, which already had concrete runways, and so the last three days of the month saw the squadron undertake the move. Gibson could reflect well on the month's achievements – 13 nights operational, 128 sorties and 561 hours 55 minutes flying time with 350 tons of bombs dropped. The losses:

BREMEN, 1934
In 1939, Bremen was the tenth largest city and fourth busiest port in Germany as well as being a major centre for the aircraft industry. It was the target for 28 major bombing raids during the war and much of the city was reduced to rubble.

five aircraft, representing 3.9% of the sorties, was the lowest since the squadron became operational.

Part of the 1930's expansion, RAF Syerston opened on 1st December and was officially opened on 18th December 1940. Syerston is about six miles south-west of Newark in Nottinghamshire. The base closed again from

RAF SYERSTON TOWER
Gibson led his No.106 Squadron to RAF Syerston in 1942. The Nottinghamshire base had been opened in 1940 and in 1943 was converted to be a training base. It retained its training role until 1970 when much of the airfield was closed and it was converted to use by gliding clubs.

December 1941 until 5th May 1942, to build concrete runways. When re-opened, Syerston became part of 5 Group and when No.106 Squadron arrived, No 61 Squadron already occupied it.

By this stage of the war some squadron commanders had become known to their men as "Francois" because they rostered themselves to fly only when the squadron was attacking the much more lightly defended French raids. Gibson was no such commander being prepared to attack the Nazi's European hegemony anywhere in Europe. The next mission was to Cologne, a target with heavy flak, and Gibson flew one of the 289 aircraft that attacked it on 15th October.

The Cologne raid was not a great success: as well as the flak there was cloud over the target and the weather forecast had not anticipated the winds. The Pathfinders had difficulty marking the target well enough to ensure a large fire did not decoy the bombers, but it did indeed attract many bombs. Gibson bombed from 11,000 feet within the squadron range of 11-12,500 feet, recording that while his bombs hit east of the river this was also when the Germans hit his aircraft. Indeed German gunnery was so accurate that the squadron lost three of the four aircraft they were to lose in the whole month of October on this raid alone. For Bomber Command the losses on this raid were 6.1% or 18 aircraft, which consideration will be relevant in later discussions on the Dambuster Raid and Harris' ambivalence towards it.

Harris had long been aware that the large Schneider works at Le Creusot in east-central France was an important target. However standing orders were that targets in France could be attacked only if zero or at least light civilian casualties could be guaranteed. This usually meant hitting targets outside of towns, or bombing by clear moonlight. Le Creusot was in a town centre, which meant the target could be attacked only in daylight. On 17th April 1942, Harris had authorised a daylight attack on a factory at Augsburg, but had lost seven of 12 Lancasters. This was deemed an unacceptable loss rate. Nevertheless, Harris eventually ordered a daylight raid for Le Creusot.

The task of attacking Le Creusot was solely for 5 Group who therefore engaged in more preparatory low flying exercises across England. The plan devised by 5 Group was for the bombers to fly out over the Channel, head down the Bay of Biscay and then turn east to fly across Vichy France at very low level. It was hoped that the opposition met over Vichy France would be much lower than over Occupied France. The bombers would

55

time their flight to arrive over Le Creusot as dusk approached. After bombing they would climb for height and head direct back to England under cover of darkness.

Setting off around mid-day from Syerston, on 17th October 1942, the No.106 Squadron contingent congregated with others in the sky above Upper Heyford before heading out to sea. Crossing the French coast just south of the Ile d'Yeu, and flying at low level the force flew some 330 miles inland arriving at Le Creusot just after 6pm - a little before dusk. Soaring to between 2,500 and 7,500 feet the Lancasters, led by Wing Commander Slee of 49 Squadron, dropped over a hundred tons of High Explosive (HE) and nearly 40 tons of incendiary bombs in less than 10 minutes.

Gibson, who had a cine camera aboard his aircraft, however, commanded six Lancasters selected to drop nearly 10 tons of HE bombs on the nearby Montchanin power station. The detail successfully accomplished their mission strafing the station and bombing from between 150 and 800 feet. Gibson bombed from 500 feet, receiving a few bullet holes, and on the raid F/Lt Hopgood made the lowest attack at only 150 feet, perhaps not surprisingly damaging his own aircraft in the process! All but one Lancaster made it home, no German fighters attacked the aerial armada in either direction - altogether there was more danger from birds with four aircraft damaged and two men injured by bird strikes. Gibson himself landed at Oakington, after a round trip of some 1,700 miles and a 10 hour 25 minute flight.

Operationally the raid was a logistical success, demonstrating targets needed defending - and probably lifting the morale of the non-collaborating French seeing an airborne armada sweeping imperiously in during daylight. However, while Gibson's mission was a complete success, as he later recorded in his flight log-book "this transformer was later reported to be destroyed and would take two years to repair", the heroic efforts of 5 Group were not wholly successful. Later PRU photographs showed much of the bombing had overshot and landed on employee accommodation with the result that most of the Schneider works had been left standing. Nevertheless, as Harris said in part of his congratulatory message, "The timing and navigation to within one minute and less than one mile over a course of 2,000 miles and the landing of one hundred aircraft in darkness under bad weather conditions on strange bases without bending a rivet evidence a standard of airmanship throughout your command which has yet to be surpassed."

New Target
New Direction

The war took another direction for No.106 Squadron when, on 22nd October 1942, they went to Italy for the first time. British belief was that the Italian appetite for the war was satiated and there was internal discontent with Mussolini's regime. Furthermore, the Eighth Army Offensive at El Alamein was due to commence on the day after this raid. Accordingly the RAF sent 112 Lancasters from 5 Group, with Pathfinders, on a bombing mission to Genoa. Typically, Gibson led his nine colleagues from the front enduring an exceptionally long flight and crossing the Alps, more successfully

LE CREUSOT AFTER RAID
This propaganda photo was issued after the Le Creusot Raid by the British government to illustrate the extent of the damage inflicted on the target. Although the target was badly damaged, not all the bombing was accurate and several French houses were destroyed.

than Hannibal, to arrive at Italy. Gibson himself bombed 1¼ miles from the aiming point, his squadron being similarly effective, as were the full bomber force, which dropped 180 tons of bombs causing heavy damage to the centre and eastern areas.

Long-range flying, over mountains, in 1942 and earlier was far from common-place and this was truly an epic mission and an heroic feat of flying. No Lancasters were lost on the raid and, after a nine hour flight, Gibson touched down at Manston to refuel recording he went on to Chelverston for breakfast before returning to base. The raid was also a success with contemporary local reports commenting on a severe effect on morale, confirming the British assessment.

The following day, 24th October, Gibson and nine others from No.106 Squadron joined 88 Lancasters in a daylight raid on the industrial city of Milan. Flying in a direct route over France and rendezvousing at Lake Annecy, the Alps were again crossed and Milan reached in broad daylight with cloud at 9-10/10 at 5-6,000 feet and clear visibility below. The raid caught the Italians by surprise, sirens went off after the first explosions, and AA defences were weak. Because of Italian unpreparedness, 135 tons of bombs fell in 18 minutes, and many of the bombers took photographs that showed the aiming point.

Gibson, who bombed from just below cloud level, may have recorded the Alps were a stunning view on the journey but the Axis Powers had to contend with the stunning realisation, following earlier attacks on Le Creusot and Genoa, that Allied aircraft were now capable of mass formation daylight raids across much of Europe as well as night-time offensives.

Milan was a success. A large number of commercial and industrial buildings, including the Caproni aircraft factory, received hits.

Despite appalling UK weather cancelling many raids throughout October, No.106 Squadron operated on eight nights and two days doing 95 sorties and 629 hours operational flying. Gibson, who recorded in his memoir he went out on four raids, again above the average he was to later claim for himself of one operation in five. The administration demands surrounding so few raids simply meant Gibson had more time to fly, although by now he was also a familiar sight at 5 Group headquarters.

In November Gibson was only operational against Italy starting with a raid on Genoa on 6th November before, on 18th November, going on to a new target: Turin. Largely selected because of the Fiat works, Turin was a medium-sized raid of 77 aircraft. In clear visibility Gibson, and seven others from his squadron, contributed to the success of the raid - four of his squadron hitting the aiming point - the rest being within two miles (Gibson himself was accurate to within a mile, which still meant his incendiaries hit the target and fell across factory buildings).

Indeed Turin was a successful raid for the RAF as a whole since the Fiat works took direct hits, as did the city centre. At this date Fiat was working on a new fighter, the Centauro. Again the raid was a feat of endurance for all - Gibson recorded seven hours twenty-five minutes flying time in his log-book and the ORB of Middle Wallop records Gibson landing short of fuel and suggests that it had not been an easy arrival.

Gibson was "Gazetted" for his D.S.O. two days after Turin, on 20th November although the station log had already recorded the award on the 10th - the list however went to the King for approval on 15th November 1942. The D.S.O. citation read:

"Since being awarded a Bar to the Distinguished Flying Cross, this officer has completed many sorties, including a daylight raid on Danzig and an attack at Gdynia. In the recent attack on Le Creusot, Wing Commander Gibson bombed and machine-gunned the transformer station nearby from 500 feet. On 22nd October, 1942, Gibson participated in the attack on Genoa and, two days later, he led his squadron in a daylight sortie against Milan. On both occasions, Wing Commander Gibson flew with great distinction. He is a most skilful and courageous leader whose keenness has set a most inspiring example."

Gibson was not involved in the second raid on Turin but did take part in the third raid on 28th November. Both the second and third raids on Turin were significantly bigger than the first effort, at 232 and 228 aircraft respectively. Although part of this force bombed before the Pathfinders had arrived, the bombing was accurate and included hits on the Royal Arsenal. On this trip Gibson had a supernumerary on his crew - Major Mullock, 5 Group's FLO - and also records cine camera film was taken as, characteristically not averse to staying over a target, Gibson flew across it several times to record the success. This Turin raid was also the raid when Gibson and F/Lt Whamond, both of No.106 Squadron, dropped the first 8,000lb bombs on Italy.

So November was a successful month for Gibson's command with 651 operational flying hours across 73 sorties, not a single aircraft was lost in the month for the first time since January 1941. Whilst the total tonnage of bombs dropped, at 155, was down - due in no small part to the number of Italian raids - the squadron was steadily climbing the accuracy league.

December 1942 was a bad month for weather at Syerston - enough that Gibson saw 16 operations cancelled and a mission recalled. Because of the poor weather Gibson himself flew no operations, and indeed was only airborne three times during the whole of December. The squadron recorded its first loss of the month, over the heavy-manufacturing centre and inland port of Duisburg, on 20th December, and with two more losses that month recorded 5.5% loss when only 54 sorties over six nights were undertaken.

The New Year of 1943 saw Bomber Command again increase their war effort. The navigational aid Oboe had been trialled in 1942 and the new H2S would improve range and ability. Meanwhile, bombing accuracy was being further assisted by the arrival of the new cascading Target Indicator Bombs, which owed so much to the fireworks industry. The specially trained

LANCASTER SQUADRON TAKES OFF, 1943
By 1943 the sight of a parade of Lancaster lining up to take off as dusk approached was a common one at bomber bases across Britain. Gibson at No.106 Squadron was one of the more active commanding officers, taking part in more raids than was usual and frequently going to Germany.

Pathfinders were to become a Group within Bomber Command on 8th January 1943, and improved aircraft continued to arrive.

5 Group alone, now entirely equipped with Lancasters, had the capability to deliver more tonnage in a night than the whole of Bomber Command had been able to achieve only a year earlier. Bomber Command was also able to put more aircraft into the line: ignoring the special exigencies surrounding the Thousand Bomber Raids in 1942, 250 bombers was a major assault. By early 1943 a major bomber assault could produce around 450 bombers - and each four-engine bomber allowed a 2¼-ton average bomb-load compared to the hitherto average of one ton with earlier aircraft. However this did not automatically mean effective use of the new technology for, after promising trials on Germany, the RAF received new orders by mid January.

The Casablanca Conference in January 1943 had declared that the RAF and the USAAF goal was to progressively disrupt and destroy the military, industrial and economic, structure of Germany, while along the way undermining morale to help reduce the ability of Germany to fight. A priority list of targets had been set but, as is the way with these conferences, the words crafted to ensure unity were sufficiently imprecise as to allow those tasked with executing the priorities considerable leeway. Faced by problems with weather, training and maintenance, Harris was happy to exploit the leeway as much as he could. Very often, however, his orders from the RAF high command were sufficiently precise to give him no chance to make his own decisions.

The U-Boat menace again raised its head and, once again, Bomber Command received orders to achieve what the Navy could not. Harris received orders to area bomb operational U-Boat bases in France - bases that, as Harris pointed out, had thick bomb-proof concrete shelters and where secondary support was now in out-lying villages. French civilian casualties were bound to be high and results low. Harris was over ruled. As a result, during the first four months of 1943, 63% of American bombs fell on U-boat related targets, Harris managing to exercise ingenuity to keep the total in this wasted exercise to some 30%. There was great destruction in many places, but the U-boats were often the only ones not affected. Accordingly, when the futility was realised, attacking U-Boats except on the open seas, dropped down the priority table from first to seventh.

That said Gibson started the New Year with some bombing trials before setting off for Essen on a Pathfinder-led mission as part of the Oboe trials. Indeed Essen had been attacked on quite small experimental Oboe guided raids on 3rd/4th, 4th/5th, 7th/8th, 9th/10th January before Gibson joined 71 other Lancasters on 11th January.

The weather on the Essen raid of 11th January was 10/10 cloud with cloud tops estimated at 15-20,000 feet. Consequently the results of this particular raid were unclear but all of Gibson's squadron recorded bombing the target flares as directed and within six minutes. Despite this being an Oboe raid, and one in which all the No.106 Squadron crews commented on poor visibility, only Gibson bombed from 2,000 feet, the rest of the squadron averaging 20,000 feet. Perhaps less heroically Gibson records in his log-book that on this mission he had left his R/T on transmit with "result very embarrassing" recorded in his log. By transmitting continuously he had blocked the radio channel for all other aircraft. It was an elementary error that would have disgraced a pilot on his first mission. Bomber Command attacked Essen on the following 10 days, which then concluded the Oboe trials.

During the "U-Boat phase" some raids on Germany still took place because Harris, and the RAF, knew the value of public opinion in reinforcing their position within the councils of war. It was also deemed necessary as if the RAF had abandoned Germany altogether, the Germans could have shifted their defences to cover the U-boats. One of these raids on Germany was to enter the history books. The BBC was keen for their star reporter, Major Richard Dimbleby, to take part in a bombing mission and broadcast to the nation. The RAF wanted the target to be a German one, and no target had a higher propaganda value than Berlin. It was almost inevitable that Gibson, by then having done an amazing 66 operations for Bomber Command, should fly him.

Whilst clearly the capital of the Reich, Berlin was also significant in the industrial German war effort: some half of the Wehrmacht's field artillery; locomotive works, small-arms and ammunition factories as well as aircraft factories were located there. Berlin was continental Europe's focal point for air transport, also where a dozen railway lines converged, whilst Greater Berlin employed about 10% of Germany's industrial workers. North Berlin had heavy machine works; the North West was full of scientific and military

DSO
The Distinguished Service Order (DSO) is a medal awarded for heroic leadership under fire and is generally regarded as a "near miss" for a Victoria Cross. Gibson was awarded his DSO in November 1942, adding the bar the following year.

installations and some aircraft plants – all targets easily argued as encapsulated within the Casablanca Directive

When both the RAF and the Luftwaffe each lacked heavy bombers it was a shorter range for the Germans to reach London from their side of the channel than it was for the British to reach Berlin from their side. RAF Hampdens had hit the German capital early in the war but the raids in retaliation for the bombing of London, including those Gibson had been on, were largely ineffective and costly. British raids had proved bombing Berlin could be done but not that it could be done well. The Luftwaffe had shown they could bomb London for 67 consecutive nights, between 7th September and 13th November 1940, the RAF had not even bombed Berlin 67 times.

Indeed post-war research suggests that Bomber Command on average killed 219 Germans and destroyed 120 German buildings a month between October 1940 and February 1942, which was significantly less than the Germans did during the 67-day bombing of London alone. Since the first Berlin raid on 25th August 1940, Bomber Command had done nine more raids in 1940–41 culminating in a large November raid of 169 aircraft. Only some 73 bombers had hit the general area of Berlin for a 12.1% loss. Despite the heroism shown, the RAF had ceased missions against Berlin as such losses were self-evidently unsustainable. The RAF therefore knew this new mission had much depending on it.

Dimbleby arrived at Syerston on 10th January 1943 along with Stanley Richardson to become versed in their role. On 16th January, 201 aircraft – 190 Lancasters and 11 Halifaxes – formed the first all four-engined bomber raid on Berlin, and the first one using target indicator ground markers. Berlin was however beyond the range of location finding aids such as Gee (where the navigator calculated his position by measuring the time taken to receive pulse signals received from three different ground stations) and Oboe.

Despite worse than expected weather and considerable cloud cover, Gibson and eight others from his squadron reported they succeeded in

GIBSON AND CREWS OF 106 SQUADRON

A staged progaganda photo issued by the British government in 1943 shows Gibson and some of his crews celebrating a successful raid on a German target. The squadron's Manchester bombers can be seen in the background.

bombing the target with several large fires taking hold. There was qualified Pathfinder success; the No.106 Squadron pilots reported seeing the red marker flares but not the white warning flares. Gibson himself was characteristically determined, doing three runs over the city whilst his bomb-aimer, Sub-Lieutenant Muttrie, located the Target Indicator (TI) and released the 8,000 lb bombs.

The raid was in one way a success because only one aircraft was lost, but the bombing was scattered across Berlin, the largest concentration being in the Templhof district, which destroyed the largest covered hall in Europe. The phenomenal achievement of one lost aircraft was no doubt in part because the RAF had not been to Berlin in 14 months and, as a result, half the flak and searchlight crews were away on a course. The air-raid warnings had been inadequate also, only announcing when the first bombs were dropping. The Gauleiter of Berlin, none other than senior Nazi propagandist in chief Josef Goebbels, was severely concerned.

The following day Dimbleby made his broadcast bringing home to the nation, and perhaps more especially those citizens who had endured bombing in their homes, that Germany was now reaping what it had sown. Dimbleby, who had overcome air-sickness because of Gibson's lateral rolling style of flying, described Gibson as "cool as a cucumber".

January was a month when Gibson flew on only two of the 13 nights the squadron operated – a doubling of the squadron's efforts of January 1942. These 13 operations translated into 611 hours over 109 sorties and the squadron achieving its 2000th sortie. Less satisfactorily, four aircraft were lost across the month.

Gibson was increasingly at 5 Group HQ restlessly pressing for different ways of doing things so his next operation was not until St Valentine's Day when Bomber Command helped show the Axis powers much toughness and little love. Whilst 243 aircraft raided Cologne, 142 Lancasters went to Milan in good visibility. At Milan No.106 Squadron achieved a record in 5 Group by taking six photographs on the aiming point – the other three aircraft, including Gibson's, being very close. Having been within 1¼ miles of the aiming point Gibson flew his aircraft over the target for 20 minutes, his crew taking more pictures.

The Milan raid was a great success, vouchsafed by experienced crews reporting fires were visible from 100 miles. Milan, with factories such as

Breda, Pirelli, Isotta-Fraschini and Alfa Romeo, received heavy damage. Perhaps more unfortunately, La Scala received bomb damage and most of the monastery of Santa Maria delle Grazie was obliterated, though fortunately the wall on which was painted Leonardo da Vinci's Last Supper mural survived.

During flight training for the month Gibson recorded trials of his own new bomb-sight and his squadron played host to the B.B.C. journalist who wanted a view of life within Bomber Command – again the RAF decided Guy Gibson and No.106 Squadron were essential to promote Bomber Command's credentials.

Whilst the February Bomber Command priority remained officially centred on the naval bases there were still some raids to Germany and Gibson took part in an historic raid on Nuremburg, a city important in Nazi history. In all 337 aircraft attacked Nuremburg on 25th February in a raid Gibson described as "good but frightening". The Pathfinders arrived late and so bombers were circling the general area, with many reporting near misses, while they waited. Within his squadron Gibson again bombed from the lowest level, by some 3,000 feet, in an attack that swiftly overwhelmed the defences.

The Nuremburg raid was more than just a psychological success. Despite much of the concentration being to the northern edges of Nuremburg there were many fires and bomb-bursts recorded by the RAF, and confirmed by the German records that reported over 300 buildings damaged in a raid with 2.7% losses of aircraft for Bomber Command.

The following day Gibson was off to Cologne again – one of 427 aircraft raiding a city "now showing signs of life after its previous heavy batterings" as the No.106 Squadron ORB had it. Gibson and his squadron all claimed to hit the green or red TI marker bomb through a slight ground haze with concentrated fires and some bursts observed. Although the opposition was recorded as heavy and accurate on this, Gibson's 70th bombing mission as reported in the Station ORB and "my 169th" war flight in his flight log-book, losses were 2.9% and none for No.106 Squadron.

The raid was essentially a success – the air raid sirens going off a bit before 9pm. By this date the new De Havilland Mosquito bomber was entering service, and was much utilised by the Pathfinders. Its combination of speed and endurance made it ideal for the role. This night, however, things went wrong. three of the four Mosquitoes carrying Oboe navigational aids and loaded with red TI markers suffered functionality issues and four of six H2S sets on the pathfinder aircraft carrying green flares not working, the red flare was dropped accurately and the green flares covered it. Twenty-one minutes later Gibson swept in straight and fast at 16,000 feet with an indicated air speed of 220 mph, hitting close to the aiming point. Later in the raid the Germans decoyed aircraft towards the south-western suburbs that, with far from atypical "creep-back", meant some bombs fell in open countryside.

In February the squadron logged 723 operational flying hours over 117 sorties losing five aircraft being 4.3% of the sorties flown.

On 11th March 1943, Wing Commander Gibson DSO DFC* went to Stuttgart, location of aircraft plants and the Bosch magneto factory, for the final mission of his second tour. Gibson wrote that he was looking forward to an anticipated holiday with Eve in Cornwall but, as ever, he continued to be resolute and did not slacken off. Three hundred and fourteen aircraft took

DA VINCI'S 'LAST SUPPER' IN MILAN
The Italians, along with most combatants, moved artistic treasures to hiding places far from likely bombing targets, but some could not be moved. Leonardo da Vinci's *Last Supper* was a mural in a monastery in Milan. It suffered a near miss and suffered slight damage when the monastery was hit on 15 August 1943.

part in the raid with 11 from No.106 Squadron. Ultimately, of the No.106 contingent, one did not take off, and one returned with W/T failure.

Crossing the enemy coast flak hit Gibson's aircraft on the far from insignificant outer starboard engine. On this Stuttgart raid Gibson was initiating a new Canadian Pilot Officer, Walter Thompson, on his first operation. Thompson later wrote in his memoirs that he assumed, as Gibson throttled the engine back, that they would head for home. Thompson records and recalls the exchange as being "We'll probably have to attack from below 15,000 feet bomb aimer. Any problems?"Thompson recalled that the bomb-aimer, Sub Lt Muttrie, clearly sharing Gibson's 'can do' attitude merely replied "No problem Sir". Gibson took his Lancaster down to 4,000 feet and pressed on until he went to 12,000 feet to make his bombing run. At 23.30 the crew dropped their bombs near a concentration of fire and Gibson headed for home.

Gibson comments the main raid hit south-west of the intended target – he himself was four miles away from the aiming point and far from alone in that. With weather over the target two to five tenths cloud in two layers at 6,000

COLOGNE
Gibson and No.106 Squadron bombed the city repeatedly to destroy its industrial capacity to produce weapons of war. Although the city centre was virtually destroyed, the vast 13th century cathedral remained almost unscathed.

and 18,000 feet, with some ground haze hampering visibility, visual identification was not easy. By the time the bombers arrived, the Pathfinder flares had mainly burnt out so most of the crews elected to bomb fire concentrations, although this was the first raid where the Germans seem to have made widespread use of dummy or decoy tactics. At this stage these were composed mostly of lighting large bonfires in open country to attract bombs, but later would become much more sophisticated with the Germans lighting their own flares to mimic those dropped by the pathfinders, building dummy towns and much else besides.

Three days later, with his leave already cancelled, Gibson transferred from No.106 Squadron – where Holden then took command, and eventually followed by John Searby through to Leonard Cheshire, who would cross paths with Gibson again. A fortnight later, on 21st March, the Squadron ORB recorded Gibson had been awarded a Bar to his DSO. Issued on 29th March the citation papers for Gibson's Bar to his DSO read:

"This officer has an outstanding operational record, having completed 172 sorties. He has always displayed the greatest keenness and, within the past 2 months, has taken part in 6 attacks against well defended targets, including Berlin. On 11th March, 1943, he captained an aircraft detailed to attack Stuttgart. On the outward flight engine trouble developed but he flew on to his objective and bombed it from a low level. This is typical of his outstanding determination to make every sortie a success. By his skilful leadership and contempt for danger he has set an example which has inspired the squadron he commands."

If the Stuttgart raid itself was a disappointment despite Gibson's own heroic flight in his usual determined manner, Gibson left the squadron on a high point. Commenting on his departure the squadron ORB said, "He commanded No.106 Squadron during a very successful year and he himself took part in all of the more important raids. He temporarily retires from active operational flying with a very remarkable record – 72 bombing sorties and 199 flying hours as a night-fighter pilot"

Of Gibson's command the indefatigable Charles Martin, No.106's Station Adjutant, a winner of the MC in World War I who had done 20 operations as a Wellington rear-gunner and a man with a Wisden-style mania for statistics, recorded a new high point. "March was without doubt one of the most successful months the squadron has yet enjoyed since being equipped with Lancaster aircraft. The September 1942 'highest' was easily exceeded, three new records being established – 350 tons of mines and bombs were dropped, 134 sorties were flown representing 834 hours of operational flying. The squadron lost only four aircraft which represent 2.9% of the month's sorties and which keeps the percentage loss over a period of 2½ years operating at 4.1%."

Gibson was C/O at No.106 Squadron for no more than a year. 'Boy Emperor' Gibson may have been to some but he was a C/O who made a difference and he won admirers. Air Vice Marshal Ralph Cochrane, commander of 5 Group, later wrote, "At this time he had reached operational maturity and the quiet forcefulness of his character permeated the whole squadron, although it must be admitted that his relations with his aircrews had a special intimacy which he was never quite able to achieve with the groundcrews." Under Gibson's leadership No.106 Squadron significantly improved its accuracy in bombing and demonstrated he was a 'hard charger' leading his squadron by example and from the front whenever there was a fresh challenge.

However Gibson was no reckless leader with a disregard for his men. The Station Operations Room Logbook several times records Gibson resisting instructions from Group HQ when he saw the interest of the men and the squadron needed it. For example, Gibson declined to send nine Lancasters nor any new men to a target on 20th April 1942. Arguing about the number of new men may not sound significant, but it was in contravention of Harris' own stated views wherein a crew should undertake only one "trial run" before being considered fit to face any target.

Indeed, at the memorial service for the, by then, Air Vice Marshal Gus Walker, long after the war, the, by then, Air Commodore John Searby recalled Gibson could be difficult to handle. However Walker, who was then the Station Commander, could always placate Gibson when he was questioning and railing at the folly of orders from HQ, and whilst all ranks throughout the ages have questioned the wisdom of their superiors, Gibson was the sort who was prepared to try and mitigate what he saw as errors.

Gibson was firmly of the view that training was important – he put training hours in himself and expected it of others – he was not for risking lives needlessly. Indeed the May Operations Room Logbook records "1030 W/C Gibson says he would like to put up Freshmen on a Gardening Trip.

Gp say can he put up 6 experienced crews for main effort instead – "no"!" The exclamation point in the ORB suggests that a refusal was clearly not expected from a C/O to his superiors. Gibson was clearly as concerned about experienced crews as much as Freshmen.

Flight Sergeant Albert Bracegirdle recalled Gibson's concern for experienced crews when he went to see Gibson about his crew not having had any leave in over six months since arriving at Syerston upon leaving O.T.U. In theory aircrew were supposed to get a week's leave every six

BOMBER HARRIS, 1943
Sir Arthur "Bomber" Harris (right) took over RAF Bomber Command in 1942 and remained in office to the end of the war. Harris's single-minded determination to destroy the Reich's ability to produce weapons and ammunition defined the activities of RAF Bomber Command.

months. Gibson summoned their flight commander, John Searby, who said Group had been calling for "maximum effort". Bracegirdle and crew instantly received leave passes. After the war, Bracegirdle went on record calling Gibson a "fair man".

Walter Thompson also commented on Gibson's regard for his crews pointing out that Gibson personally took him up as a second pilot for his first raid, and ensured a personal introduction to the pilot Thompson would be flying with on his next operation – since Gibson was posted out and unable to take him up again. Thompson, after the war, recalled Gibson as a man for whom "because there was a war on was no reason for lapses of courtesy, warmth and modest behaviour".

Thompson also commented "Too, if the operation was a dangerous one, Gibson's name would head the flying list..." which Thompson can only have known by hearsay given his short time at the Squadron with Gibson, and suggests that that was the general belief expressed in conversation. As we have seen this is true whenever No.106 Squadron had untested raids, or even unexpected Gardening missions where Freshmen crews were not prepared. Gibson would lead from the front and put himself in harm's way. In "Enemy Coast Ahead" Gibson opined a Squadron Commander with all those inherent responsibilities would only do an operation every five nights – there were months when Gibson did more.

Of course Gibson had his detractors, and probably acquired more as his legend grew. Possibly recalling his C/O in the demoralised under-performing 29 Squadron, Gibson was a stern disciplinarian believing it under-pinned professionalism. Gibson could be the life and soul of the party and was partial to a drink as so many young men are, let alone young men at war, but there was no drinking before an operation and strict formality when on duty. Gibson had a drive to succeed, a drive that is unlikely to be present in all and so that too could cause some to feel resentful. After all Gibson had much to be confident about – an outstanding record, the eye of Harris, and frankly, that he had survived.

Gibson's record speaks for itself as C/O. He wrote well of his men when he left, and as ever spoke of the importance of ground crews, but it was Gibson who led them to a stronger position. As so often this would not earn Gibson a rest but would require more of him: his greatest challenge and one that would make him a household name for heroism.

Top Secret
Preparations

Gibson had completed another tour with Bomber Command and now, as an acting Wing Commander, a posting to O.T.U. would have been typical. Unexpectedly, however, on 15th March 1943, Gibson was posted to 5 Group HQ at Grantham, his leave was cancelled and John Searby took over as C/O of No.106 Squadron.

Already there was emerging talk of Gibson writing a book, to help the RAF attract people to and motivate those within the service, and promote to other members of society the value of the RAF. However, Gibson's duties

NO.617 SQUADRON LANCASTER
One of several Lancaster bombers that were specially converted for use by No.617 Squadron on the Dams Raid. The large and unwieldy bomb release mechanism was located in the centre of the aircraft, leaving no room for the dorsal gun turret that was removed.

73

officially were that he should be "setting down his thoughts on bomber tactics". Having contributed, as Cochrane later wrote, towards a "pre-eminence which the squadron had attained under his leadership, and his own exceptional contribution of 172 sorties" it was hardly a surprising assignment. Perhaps the assignment was even predictable in light of Gibson's experience and all the regular trips he had made to Grantham during his command of No.106 Squadron when seeking a better way of doing things.

Within two days, in which Gibson gives the impression he was not a natural "fit" in HQ at Grantham, Air Vice Marshal Cochrane, Air Officer Commanding 5 Group, approached Gibson and asked him to undertake one more important operational raid. That Gibson would agree to do a raid, an important one, and therefore probably an atypical one must have been predictable. However it was less predictable that the target details would be kept secret from him for quite some time.

As far back as September 1937 the Air Ministry had considered German reservoirs and dams as potential targets. The Möhne and Sorpe dams between them provided about 70% of the water for the Ruhr's industrial purposes as well as all the drinking water for the four and a half million inhabitants. With the Ruhr Valley only twenty miles away, the hydro-electric power generating capacity was significant. The nearby Eder Dam held back more water than the Möhne in capacity, and was the biggest dam in Germany.

Plans to destroy these and other dams had been hampered by the lack of a weapon powerful enough to destroy the massive dams, yet light enough to be carried by an aircraft. After what must have seemed endless delays, false starts and bureaucratic paperwork, the answer was found late in 1942 by aviation engineer Barnes Wallis. Even so, Harris was dubious about the idea and more delays ensued before the mission was given the go-ahead.

Having been posted to 5 Group on 15th March, and agreeing another return to operational flying as well as being given the unpecedented power to choose his entire Squadron, Gibson led to the formation of the Squadron on 17th March with Gibson as its C/O – his second and final operational squadron command. At first the speed was such that the squadron had no official name, being referred to as "Squadron X". Only later did it acquire the designation of No.617 Squadron.

Two days later Gibson was back at Scampton, for the second time in his career, to a party at the mess – whisky for him, beer for Nigger! The nature of the No.617 Squadron team was later to become an international promotional dream for the RAF and the Air Ministry for it was a truly international squadron. From his own former command Gibson picked Hopgood and Shannon the Australians; and Burpee a Canadian; Joe MCarthy from Brooklyn an American; Les Munro from New Zealand; Mick Martin as well as Jack Leggo, Les Knight, Len Chambers, Toby Foxley, Bob Hay from Australia. Of the 133 aircrew who flew the raid, 89 were British, 28 Canadian, 13 Australian, two New Zealanders, and one American. Naturally, this meant they were members of many air-forces: 12 from RAAF, 27 RCAF, 2 RNZAF, 92 RAF, but, as Gibson said, "Nearly all of them twenty-three years old or under, and nearly all of them veterans".

The Squadron began gathering at Scampton on 21st March, two days later it was decided to convert 23 Lancasters. On 21st March 1943, No.617 Squadron officially came into existence (the ORB says "was formed on 24th March 1943", the ORB for Station Sick Quarters at Scampton recording on 4th April 1943 "No 617 Squadron commenced to form as a new Squadron this month and is not, as yet, a complete Squadron"). The crews, using ten borrowed Lancasters, began intensive training before the end of the month. The Squadron still did not know the targets but did know it was to be a low-level operation at night and practiced low-level formation flying, as well as building up their team working. That the crew needed to work together, even more than usual, was clear in the Operational Orders where "aircraft are to use the method of attack already practiced. The pilot being responsible for line, the Navigator for height, the Air Bomber for range and the Flight Engineer for speed". The flights practiced by the new squadron involved routes to Eyebrook reservoir two miles south of Uppingham between Leicestershire and Rutland; Abberton reservoir south-west of Colchester, Essex; and the Derwent reservoir in Derbyshire.

Back in London, at the Air Ministry in King Charles Street, a meeting on 25th March discussed the name for the operation. The next code in the Bomber Command block of codes being "Chastise", that was selected although notification of this was not passed on from 5 Group to the Officer Commanding at Scampton until 16th May – the operation rejoicing in the not very catchy description "Operational order No.B 976" until then. The special bombs were codenamed "Upkeep", with "Highball" being the designation given to smaller versions intended for use against smaller targets.

The 25th March meeting was also the one, which, because of the calculation about water capacity in the dams, made the Air Ministry set 26th May as the last date for operations because, "it is doubtful whether the water levels in the dams will be sufficiently high in the June moon period to offer a reasonable prospect of success".

The first modified Lancaster arrived at the station on 18th April. Apart from bomb bay modifications, fuselage strengthening at the bomb bay,

ABBERTON RESERVOIR
This reservoir in Essex was used by No.617 Squadron to practise for the Dams Raid as it was of a similar shape and size to the lake held back by the Eder Dam, the second target of the great raid.

installation of a motor to spin the bomb, and the removal of a lot of armour, the most significant change was the removal of the mid-upper turret. Many of the Lancaster modifications were to assist in reducing the aeroplane's weight, which was essential to offset the increased bomb weight with the consequent impact on the fuel needed to fly the mission.

In his typical breezy style Gibson recalls two close shaves with death nearly being killed twice in only two days: not over the Ruhr but the viciousness of Margate! On the first day Gibson and the Senior Air Staff Officer (SASO), Bob Hay were strolling in Margate waiting for summons to the tests when four FW 190s strafed and bombed the town. On 11th April Gibson and Hay took off in a single engine Magister aircraft to return to Scampton. When they were about 300 feet above Margate the engine stopped. As Gibson later wrote, "When an engine stops in a four-engine aircraft you don't have to worry too much - but when it happens in a single-engine aircraft, then the long finger of gravity points toward Mother Earth – and so we began coming down!"

Being in southern England, the anti-invasion defences around Kent and Essex were quite intense – mainly consisting of anti-landing devices. Gibson drifted towards Birchington, finally crashlanding in the field at the top of Brooksend Hill, just beyond the last houses on the south side of the road. The RAF rescue unit from Manston arrived shortly afterwards, but not until after a local policeman had taken details and praised the effectiveness of the anti-landing equipment! The Magister wreckage was recovered within a few days, but this remains significant as the only crash-landing Gibson ever made.

The flight training was vigorous and, as ever, Gibson was exacting in his standards. The RAF, requiring reports on everything ordered a weekly summary of training reports to be written from the C/O of the squadron based there at Scampton to the Scampton station commander also based there, which he then précised and sent to London! The Report dated 16th April 1943 reported, "Flight Sergeant Lovell, from No.57 squadron, did not come up to the standard necessary for this Squadron and was replaced by Sgt Divall, from the same Squadron". The intensity of the training is clear when the report goes on to opine that Divall, obviously behind the others in flying "should catch up by the end of next week". The same report also points out that, with Gibson being "attached to Manston", Young was also not getting much flying in.

Meanwhile, testing of the bomb was not going well. The third trial drop of a real bomb took place on 21st April when Avro's test-pilot, Sam Brown, dropped two "spheres" in succession. The results were still not wholly satisfactory, and, at a conference in Weybridge on 24th April, Gibson agreed to the lowering of the bomb release height to 60 feet, and back in Scampton the training commenced at this new level from 26th April. No altimeter then in production could measure precisely at 60 feet and it is here that one of the few inaccuracies in the film "The Dam Busters" took place. Gibson did not have the idea of the spotlights, it was Mr Lockspeiser from the Ministry of Aircraft Production. The method saw two spotlights fitted to each Lancaster, one at the nose and one at the tail. These were aimed so that their beams met precisely 60 feet beneath the aircraft. If the spotlights did not meet the pilot was at the wrong height. Harris was appalled at the risk the lights brought to the crews. "I will not have aircraft flying about with spotlights on in defended areas ... get some of these lunatics controlled and if possible locked up", he wrote in high dudgeon. Nevertheless many crews trialled it and "all have reported most highly on its efficiency" as was reported in the weekly Report for the week ending 15th April 1943.

The squadron started practicing at 60 feet over the Eyebrook reservoir, in formations of ten from 5th May. The pace at both Manston and Scampton was relentless because the experts, having calculated that the dams would be at maximum capacity in the May moon period, also knew that the next favourable period, if action did not happen in May, would be February or March 1944. Nobody was of the opinion that secrecy about the bouncing bomb was possible for nearly another year. Additionally, in London at an Air Ministry meeting on 5th May, the AOC 5 Group commented that crews were reaching the peak of efficiency and interest which could not be upheld much longer and felt the operation should be the May moon period on or as soon after 14th May as possible.

By 6th May Bomber Command HQ were advised from Scampton "all crews are now ready to operate" with the exception of no actual Upkeep bomb dropping practice. The intention was that there would be practice Upkeeps (lacking only explosives) available in Kent between 10th and 13th May for the crews to practice with.

Squadrons need Operational Orders in the RAF and Harold Satterley sent the draft operational order for the raid on the dams to Scampton for comment on 10th May. Satterley explicitly tasked the Station Commander, Charles Whitworth, with redrafting: "Here is the draft copy of the Operation Order written, as you will see, all by my own fair hand. Will you please get down to it right away with Gibson and either re-write it completely to suit yourselves or pin it on slips of paper giving any amendments you want to suggest". Because No.617 Squadron were at Reculver on the following two days, practicing dropping inert Upkeep bombs, Gibson amended the draft operational order and returned it on 12th May.

Gibson's suggested amendments ranged from affirming target codes should be the "A B C" used in practice not "X Y Z" to technical matters. Satterley's unusually relaxed attitude towards the drafting of the order show how Gibson was seen as pivotal to the success of the raid given he was the junior officer by both rank and position.

On 13th May more of No.617 Squadron practiced at Reculver, damaging one Lancaster ironically on the very day the last expected modified Lancaster arrived at Scampton; and a prototype Lancaster was sent from Boscombe Down to Scampton for conversion. Meanwhile, at Broadstairs, the first live Upkeep bomb drop took place – and it bounced as intended. It was on 14th May that Chalres Portal, Chief of the Air Staff, signalled from Washington that Chastise was to go ahead. No.617 squadron did a full rehearsal for the raid at night with nineteen aircraft taking part.

The pace accelerated on 15th May when, with a clear instruction to de-couple the Upkeep and Chastise programmes the Air Ministry decided the Operation should be as soon as possible. With a second live Upkeep bomb being tested at Broadstairs Air Chief Marshal the Honourable Sir Ralph Cochrane, the AOC of 5 Group, advised Scampton that the operation was imminent and key personnel there received a briefing. On 16th May the decision was taken to execute Operation Chastise, the message sent to Whitworth reading, "Executive Operation Chastise 16.5.43 zero hours 22.48 B.". On the same day the "cover story" of "a mine of great size" dropped "sufficiently close to the target to be effective" was re-affirmed, along with the arrangements for handling the media.

The
Dams Raid

"Led attack on Möhne an Eder Dams. Successful" – the entirety of Gibson's log-book entry for probably the most famous raid by a single squadron in the history of war aviation.

The entry was understated, the drama was much higher. That drama had begun even before the aircraft took off. Gibson's beloved pet dog Nigger was run down and killed by a car. Distrought, Gibson left orders that the dog was to be buried at midnight, the time he was due to deliver his attack on the Möhne Dam. That way both master and pet might be going into the ground at the same time.

The operation was to be in three waves. Nine aircraft would attack the Möhne, at planning stage designated as target X. Gibson was to lead the first wave with Hopgood and Martin in his echelon. The second echelon of the Möhne wave comprised of Dinghy Young, Astell, and Maltby. The final echelon in this wave was comprised of Maudslay, Knight, and Shannon.

Those from the Möhne wave who had a bomb left were to head on and attack the Eder, target Y.

The Sorpe, target Z, was to be attacked by five aircraft who were assigned to that dam alone. Piloted by McCarthy, Rice, Munro, Byers, and Barlow this wave took a more northerly route.

The remaining five aircraft were a mobile reserve to augment any of the earlier waves or, if not needed for that, they were to attack other dams. The pilots in this active reserve were Burpee, Anderson, Townsend, Ottley, and Brown

At 21:28 Barlow took off in the first of nineteen heavily laden aircraft. Because the second wave had a longer route to fly, they were to take off first, and all five did so singly. Four were airborne within eleven minutes of Barlow taking off; the leader of the wave, McCarthy, having to switch to the spare aircraft, took off at 22:01. Incredibly this "spare aircraft" was the very last to arrive in the squadron having arrived on 16th May!

At 21:39, unusually taking off together in formation, were Gibson, flanked by Hopgood and Martin – the first echelon of the first wave as men began to pass into legend. The second formation was airborne at 21:47 and the third at 21:59.

The third wave had five aircraft airborne between 00:09 and 00:15.

Gibson was near the bend of the Rhine at Rees before he actually faced fire, from floating flak-positions and several on the shores. Intense flak close

---

THE DAM BUSTERS MOVIE
The raid to destroy the Ruhr Dams captured the public imagination at the time, and was immortalised in the form of the 1955 docu-movie *The Dam Busters*, staring Richard Todd. The film has become staple fare for British TV schedules and continues to sell well as a DVD in the 21st century.

to Dulmen damaged Hopgood's wing, and caused radio silence to be broken Gibson warning the rest of the squadron.

Flying across Europe at a low level, so low that Gibson and his echelon nearly flew into power lines and Young almost hit a house, had caused a number of navigational problems, mostly swiftly corrected. Eventually, however, the first wave echelon separated and the first to arrive at the dam was Martin, who stooged around for a bit until Hopgood and Gibson arrived.

Astell, from the second wave, was destined not to arrive, shot down in deadly cross-fire approximately where Gibson had encountered troubles, he was the first of the first wave to crash, just north-west of Dorsten at about the time Martin arrived at the Möhne.

Once he arrived at the dam, Gibson reconnoitred as he set about establishing the accuracy of the briefing information, the flak missing him as it started up. Satisfied, Gibson then went into the attack. With it clear an attack was underway, the defences were fully alert and opened up on Gibson who was flying in straight and true, his own guns blazing. Dropped accurately, at 00:28 in the bright moonlight the bomb bounced three times and, as Gibson soared upwards, the bomb exploded against the dam. When the water subsided however the wall was intact.

As Maudslay and Knight arrived, Gibson ordered Hopgood into the attack but the Germans drew a line on him; hit by flak, in both wings, on his run across the lake the Lancaster caught fire. Although successfully released, the bomb bounced over the wall and blew up the pumping station. Engulfed in flames Hopgood gallantly struggled for height to try to save his crew. At 500 feet the wing of Hopgood's aircraft dropped off and the Lancaster plunged to the ground. Through his heroic efforts three of Hopgood's crew did manage to bail out, although only two survived to become prisoners of war.

Martin was next, only ten minutes earlier Gibson had released his bomb, but Gibson wasted no time either. Gibson came in on the attack diving towards the dam, slightly ahead of Martin, and to starboard, forward guns firing, before he crossed the dam from right to left so the rear-gunner could also fire. This aerial assault by Gibson and his crew provided good cover for Martin resulting in the Germans not immediately spotting him on his approach run. The two Lancasters were flying around the dam, as many guns blazing as they could: Martin dropped accurately, the bomb veered slightly, a huge waterspout erupted - and again the dam held.

"Dinghy"Young stepped up to the attack. Gibson was not to be alone on decoy duty this time as he patrolled the other side of the dam, firing guns and switching lights on and off, to distract the Germans. Martin also joined the fray and took up formation with Young as they flew towards the dam together forward guns firing. Young joined those delivering right on target as the bomb bounced and made contact but, again, the dam held.

David Maltby prepared himself, as Gibson and Martin assumed positions either side of him. As well as all firing with their guns, Gibson and Martin switched on every light to distract further the German defences and the three Lancasters engaged the dam and its defences. Guns blazing, Merlins roaring, Maltby's Lancaster flew in. Maltby, suddenly convinced the wall was crumbling, slightly veered to his port side and released his bomb.

THE MOEHNE DAM
The first of the dams to be destroyed by No.617 Squadron was the Möhne Dam, which had a hole some 220 feet wide and 70 feet tall torn in it. The resulting torrent of water destroyed the village of Neheim and killed over 1200 people.

THE EDER DAM

The second dam to be breached during the Dams Raid was the Eder. The hole blasted here was slightly larger than that at the Möhne Dam, but the resulting wall of water that raced downstream was less destructive as the Eder Valley was not heavily populated at the time.

Maltby cleared the dam wall when the bomb went off causing another huge water-plume.

Shannon was preparing his run as Maltby, Gibson, and Martin circled the valley waiting for the water to settle. As soon as the water did settle, Shannon began his run over the now quiet waters. Before Shannon was fully committed to the run, Martin called over the radio that the dam wall was crumbling. Martin was right, the wall suddenly gave way – water surged down into the valley. Gibson sent the code word "Nigger" back to Scampton, at 00:56 letting them know of the squadron's success. In line with the plans, Gibson gave the order for those with bombs to proceed to the Eder and sent Maltby and Martin home.

Heading east the aircraft went to the Eder independently. Several aircraft had problems finding the dam, including Gibson who arrived at the reservoir too far west – whereas Shannon was further off being at the Rehbach Dam nearby. Gibson and Young (now designated deputy) were at the correct dam with no bombs, the others who had bombs were not visible in the mist. Gibson called up on the radio and established the situation – calmly firing Very lights to reveal his position to the others, and any Germans that may have been around! The Eder was undefended but it was in a narrower and steeper valley and, as is not unusual near a dam, a mist was forming. Furthermore, there had only been photographs of the Eder, no models to give a better idea of the terrain so the aircraft circled and the pilots discussed how best to attack.

Dave Shannon went in but found himself uncomfortable with the position each time and so, on Gibson's orders, stepped back to refocus himself.

Whilst Shannon flew around regaining his situational awareness, Henry Maudslay went into the attack. Maudslay too, as Shannon, overshot so came round for a second attempt. The second attempt on the dam also led to Maudslay over-shooting at which point Shannon resumed the attack. Shannon felt refocused enough to make a run, accurately dropped his bomb, and believed he caused a small breach. Releasing the bomb on his third run, Maudslay flew over the dam just as the bomb hit the top and, after the resulting explosion, Maudslay's aircraft and crew were never seen again.

Gibson, unaware of Astell's crash, called him up but, receiving no reply, it became clear that all hinged on Les Knight who had the last remaining bomb. Les Knight swept in and made a dummy run before going again, released the bomb, at 01:52, with the precision expected of a top squadron and the accuracy dreamed of by scientists where, after three bounces, the bomb made contact and the Eder dam collapsed. Sending the code word "Dinghy" at 01:54 as the water, forced into a narrower space than that of the Möhne, swept down the valley with a much greater concentration, the survivors turned for home.

Meanwhile the second wave Lancasters reached the enemy coast without significant incident until, crossing the Dutch coast light flak hit Les Munro's aeroplane. The damage to Munro's Lancaster was light but operationally significant. The flak had made Munro's intercom unserviceable and, in a low-flying operation where swift communication between the operatives, and other aircraft in the formation, was crucial there was no choice but to head for home.

Byers was the first casualty, shot down by flak when flying over Texel, it seems probable that Byers crashed at 22:57.

Geoff Rice, who had been flying so low he had to pull up to avoid sand dunes, hit the Zuyder Zee, his bomb ripped off but swift reflexes meant he managed to regain the air. However having lost his bomb, Rice too was forced to abandon the mission and return to Scampton.

Flak had hit Barlow, detonating his bomb. That left only McCarthy, who had commandeered the spare aircraft and thus taken off later than the wave he was to lead, to fly on alone to the Sorpe.

Locating the dam McCarthy, worked out a likely attack line swept in ten times and hit the dam. The dam with the construction least suited to the use of this bomb held, with the destruction of parts of the upper wall. Despite flying over the area until nearly 01:00 it was clear the dam was not breaking and McCarthy headed for Scampton.

The rest of the mobile reserve had variable fortunes. Having taken off at 00:09, flak brought Ottley down near Hamm on the way to the Lister Dam – the one survivor from the aircraft, the rear gunner Tees, later reporting searchlights had coned the aircraft and the flak gunners had been accurate. Burpee, who had left Scampton at 00:11 strayed off course and ended up flying over the Luftwaffe base of Gilze-Rijen. Not surprisingly the base was well defended and despite quickly-thinking a bluff by putting on his landing-lights Burpee was shot down – around 02:00 on the edge of the airfield. The bomb then detonated causing over a million Guilders' worth of damage to assorted buildings.

Two of the reserve aircraft went on to the Sorpe after McCarthy. Brown, who had taken off at 00:12, encountered heavy flak fire, and flew extremely low, at one point flying along a road below the level of the bordering trees, to evade the flak. Diverted to the Sorpe having seen the devastation caused by the breach in the Möhne, Brown had several goes lining up on a target which mist was rapidly covering but, by 03:14, felt it was clear enough to release the bomb and it hit the dam. Heavily attacked by flak on the way home as well Brown kept low, on maximum revs, and landed safely at Scampton.

Anderson also considered the fog too thick. The Official Report on Operation Chastise records mist in the valleys disorientated Anderson and that searchlights he could not shoot out because of power stoppages in a turret forced him off his route. Anderson decided he could not reach the target on time so turned for home at 03:10 and took his bomb back to Scampton.

Townsend diverted to the Ennepe dam, also hitting it accurately at 03:37 but with no visible results.

Since the war, there is now some doubt if Townsend had hit the Ennepe or the Bever, Townsend had reported difficulty finding the dam and in his post-raid report he had said that his map was incorrect. Given the Bever is only some five miles south-west of the Ennepe and that it has a similar topography, the confusion seems comprehensible. Contemporary German

THE SORPE DAM
The third dam to be attacked by No.617 Squadron was the Sorpe. It was hit by one bouncing bomb, but although damaged it did not collapse. Another raid in 1944 with more conventional bombs also failed to destroy it.

records reported that the Bever Dam was attacked at almost the same time as the Sorpe. Furthermore, the officials in charge of the Ennepe claim the only bomb that dropped near them in the whole war was in the woods not the water. The fact remains that Townsend pressed home an attack, in the spirit of the squadron.

Maltby was the first of the attacking aircraft to return to Scampton, at 03:11, Gibson was the third back, Townsend was the last – eight did not return. Gibson, who had flown back via the Möhne, had a relatively

GIBSON AT NO.617 SQUADRON DAMS PARTY
It was traditional in the RAF to hold a party after a major raid. Gibson can be seen bottom centre, while Barnes Wallis is to the left with white hair. Wallis was traumatised by the losses suffered by No.617 Squadron and never fully forgave himself.

uneventful flight home. To avoid a fighter Gibson went down to below tree-top level at one point but shot out at the Helder peninsula in a fast dive to reach the North Sea; the most eventful incident on his return flight being the sight of an explosion in the air above Hamm, later realised to be Ottley. Gibson landed at 04:15 at Scampton observers recalling his hair plastered down with sweat despite flying in shirt-sleeves, and his aircraft had three small holes in the tail.

Wallis was devastated; the effects indubitably stayed with him the rest of his life - his charitable giving for the RAF just one sign. In a letter to Cochrane, after the Raid, Wallis wrote, "please accept the deepest sympathy of all of us on the losses which the Squadron has sustained...for me the subsequent success was almost completely blotted out by the sense of loss of those wonderful young lives". Harris was reportedly delighted at the result, telephoning Portal in Washington so the news could be relayed to Churchill, but concerned about the level of loss – rather more, seemingly, than he had been over the similar Augsburg Raid.

So what was the outcome of the raid on the dams? The Scampton ORB recorded, "NO.617 SQUADRON OPERATED FROM SCAMPTON FOR THE FIRST TIME WITH 19 LANCASTERS. No.617 SQUADRON was formed on the 24th March 1943, and after six weeks training were detailed on the evening of 16th May to attack the German dams. 3 Lancasters were unsuccessful and returned for various reasons. 8 returned having successfully completed their task. 8 are missing of which 3 are known to have delivered attacks on their targets. As a result of this raid the Möhne and Eder Dams were breached and the structure of the Sorpe Dam seriously damaged. The attack was led by Wing Commander G.P. Gibson, D.S.O. and Bar, D.F.C. and Bar, who was awarded the Victoria Cross." The dry prose of the RAF Permanent Record is good as far as it goes but what of the raid from other perspectives?

For Bomber Command the consequences were significant. The RAF had conducted a precision raid, at low level at night – a first for aerial warfare and one that the propaganda machine was swift to exploit. The use of VHF radio, a Gibson initiative, led directly to the concept of the "Master Bomber", a commander flying over the target to direct aircraft on to a target and thereby improve accuracy. However the modified Lancasters went to storage on 26th December 1944, at the same time as storage of the unused Upkeep weapons.

The consequences for the Squadron were immediate, not least the decision to keep the squadron as a specialist unit, not disband it. Telegrams flowed in, from Trenchard, Lockspeiser, Harris, RAF Manston (slyly having a dig at Gibson crashing their Magister), C-in-C Coastal Command, Avro, AOC 5 Group, and the Secretary of State amongst others. Harris also sent a generous telegram to Wallis. Perhaps most significantly No.617 Squadron earned a Squadron Standard of Battle Honours – the youngest Squadron to achieve that distinction.

For Upkeep, the decision made was that, even whilst assessing its practicality for attacks on the German canal system, in order to safeguard the Highball programme unrestricted use could not take place. Operationally this meant that the Chiefs of Staff were, again, the arbiters of any further use. What was not immediately known after the raid on the dam, although by June Portal was speculating it was so, was that the Germans already had an intact Upkeep and had reverse-engineered it to comprehend the mechanism. However the Germans had not discovered the spinning part of the Upkeep delivery mechanism and therefore the method of operation. In fact it was not until 2nd August that the British were certain the Germans had an Upkeep weapon, and therefore felt able to ask the Chiefs of Staff for sanction to use the weapon again.

What of the men? The Official report into Gibson's leadership of the raid concluded, "All crew were unanimous in their appreciation of W/C Gibson's outstanding courage, and of his skill and coolness in leading and controlling, without which they do not believe that the operation could have been the success that it was." There were 41 medals issued because of the Dams Raid: a VC, 5 DSOs, 14 DFCs, 12 DFMs and 2 CGM. It is not generally known that the other medals issued were Iron Cross Second Class. The officer and men of the six-gun battery who showed considerable courage manning their posts while Lancasters roared out of the sky at them spitting lead and tracer, and launching an hitherto unimagined weapon at their position each earned the Iron Cross. Courage indeed knows no national boundaries. However Gibson, who was not impressed that Anderson had failed to find a target and had returned at 03:10 bringing his Upkeep with him. He swiftly had Anderson, who he felt had not completed the raid, transferred out of the squadron.

Nineteen aircraft had set out on the mission, attacking five dams, destroying two, and damaging two more. Eight aircraft were lost – 42% of the squadron, and Harris remained privately sceptical about the outcome and the price paid. Harris had presided over the much higher percentage losses on the Augsburg raid (although that was seven aircraft downed from 12 and thus a 52% loss rate), but also many raids of much less accuracy had lost more aircraft and crews. Nevertheless, Harris's response to both raids was the same – no more daylight raids at law altitudes and no more bouncing bomb raids at 50 feet – again his views on area bombing were, in his eyes, vindicated.

However what was the price for the Germans of the raid on the dams?

The consequences for the Germans are controversial now, it has become

UPKEEP IN LANCASTER
Throughout the war and for many years afterwards the actual design of "Upkeep", the codename for the bouncing bomb, was a closely guarded secret. This photo shows the bomb loaded on to a No.617 Squadron Lancaster together with the release mechanism that span the bomb as it was dropped.

fashionable to minimise the raid from the comfort of our homes in a country not facing domestic war. Albert Speer, the eminence grise of German production, set to work with his undoubted efficiency to deal with the raid's consequences. Inevitably the dam defences were increased and both dams repaired – using significant resources taken off other war work, not least the building of the walls intended for Normandy. As Speer wrote, "A few days after this attack seven thousand men, whom I had ordered shifted from the Atlantic Wall to the Möhne and Eder areas, were hard at work repairing the dams." The Germans needed a force of workers until 23rd September 1943 to rebuild just the Möhne. Those men were later returned to the war work from where they had come, but the anti-aircraft guns that were moved in to ring every dam in Germany remained for the duration.

Floods had spilled across the Ruhr, flooding mines, extinguishing furnaces swamping homes and factories. There were over 1200 people

GIBSON AND THE KING
The Dams Raid proved to be a massive propaganda coup for the RAF, and for Britain. King George VI visited RAF Scampton a few days later and was photographed with Gibson as the two men discussed the raid.

killed because of the raid. Over 6,000 acres of crops were ruined, 6,500 cattle and pigs killed, 125 factories destroyed or damaged, hundreds of miles of roads and railway swept away, 25 bridges destroyed, and production in the Ruhr dropped.

The German official Incident Report on the damage lists: six overhead power cables destroyed for lengths up to two miles, the camp erected for workers at a cost of nearly a million marks was destroyed; and 996 dead and 221 missing (of which 563 dead and 155 missing were not German). Even by the 22nd May, there were 380 of the technical emergency service; 1,250 military personnel; 102 from the Red Cross; and 150 firemen still engaged on emergency service work. Other physical losses were: 3,000 homes ruined, 25 bridges destroyed, and production in the Ruhr dropped.

The British official reports had the breach in the Eder Dam as 180 feet wide and that as a result ⅞ of the water had poured out, leaving the water level 75 feet below the crown, and concomitant damage to the power station and the compensating basin, with floods having reached Kassel. The Möhne was reported as a having a breach 230 feet wide at the top extending to the foundations, and the lake drained, with an extensive list of damaged bridges, railway lines, embankments, marshalling yards and flooded factories/works, the waters having reached Dortmund.

The Sorpe, the dam least suited to the bomb in use, came close to destruction had the bomb been lower when it exploded the water would probably have completed the job. Of the Sorpe the British Report concluded, "present evidence suggests that the structure was not seriously damaged and that no seepage is taking place". Speer wrote of the damage to this dam, "they did achieve a direct hit on the centre of the dam. I inspected it that same day. Fortunately the bomb hole was slightly higher than the water level. Just a few inches lower – and a small brook would have been transformed into a raging river which would have swept away the stone and earthen dam."

Later inspection of PRU pictures by Wallis, in February 1944, spotted a new reinforcing wall under construction on the Eder and probably the Möhne "from which we may infer that a good deal of damage was done to the parts that still remained standing". Wallis' surmise about the retaining wall was borne out, after the war, when the RAF had access to German records.

Gibson's
Final Year

Whilst Sir Archibald Sinclair was the first to announce the news, the Air Ministry communiqué followed swiftly. On 18th May, the press in the free world gave extensive coverage to the Dams Raid, with photographs of Gibson, and the dams themselves well to the fore. Predictably the nationals featured the stories, as did regional papers like the "Lincolnshire Echo" and of course local angles were played to as in the "West Briton" heading a story "Proud of her Dam Buster Grandson". Atypically for stories of the time there was no secret about the Squadron, nor the commander, with pictures and names mentioned freely.

Churchill, still in America, announced the raid as part of his speech to Congress, on 19th May receiving cheers from the Americans for his rhetoric. As Churchill said:

"Our air offensive is forcing Germany to withdraw an ever larger proportion of its war-making capacity from the fighting fronts. Hundreds of fighter aircraft, thousands of anti-aircraft cannon, and many hundreds of thousands of men, together with a vast share in the output of the war factories, have already been assigned to this purely defensive function".

If modern cynicism should consider Churchillian speeches to America as purely rhetoric designed to keep a balance between the Allies then the entire justification for the raid on the dams as a strategic policy is answered by Speer. In his speech to the workers who had rebuilt the dams Speer said, "You have in a remarkably short period of time repaired this dam, thus performing a service to the Ruhrgebeit which will be directly translated into more weapons and more munitions."

On 28th May, the awards to the men of No.617 Squadron were Gazetted, Gibson's recommendation going to the King on 22nd May and the rest of his Squadron on 26th May. The speed of the recognition was exemplary, if some of the accuracy was less so, but the legend was now growing, with so many awards for a single action.

On 28th May, the King and Queen went to Scampton to meet No.617 Squadron, at the end of a tour of other stations and lunched there.

On 22nd June, the Squadron members, and others, gathered at Buckingham Palace for the Investiture. There were some items of note about the event. With the King absent in North Africa the Queen handed over the medals, the first time a Queen had physically presented a VC since Victoria. What is more unusual Gibson received his VC at the beginning of the investiture, despite the convention that this usually happens at the end of

GIBSON WITH RCAF OF 617
The multi-national make up of No.617 Squadron air crew was seized upon by the publicists of the British government for propaganda purposes. This photo shows Gibson (arms folded) posing with the Canadians and others who had flown with him on the Dams Raid.

an investiture; and atypically the Squadron received their medals together by alphabetical order not by medal class. After the event, and taking all the permutations of photographs, Avro hosted a meal at the Hungaria Restaurant in Lower Regent Street at which Gibson received a gold cigarette case.

Gibson was too much of a celebrity for his superiors to wish him to fly operationally against the Germans; the propaganda value to them of shooting him down would have been too great. Gibson's last official flight with No.617 Squadron seems to have been on 2nd August where he and Holden undertook a flight of nearly an hour and a half.

On 3rd August Gibson officially relinquished command of No.617 Squadron, a squadron he had created, moulded, inspired with his ethos – but ironically was so successful with that he was no longer able to fly with again. Instead, capitalising on the publicity that made him too valuable to go to Germany again, Gibson was now to go on a goodwill tour of Canada and North America.

Such tours were not unusual. Nettleton, the hero of Augsburg had been on a tour in 1942 when there were concerns about the state of Anglo-American relations. From a casual idea by Secretary of State Morgenthau to the Director-General of the British Information Services in the United States and Minister designate at Washington, who had expressed concerns to the Cabinet about American perceptions of the British war effort, the idea had grown. Nettleton's tour had been a success he had gone down well, as had the others he went with – all carefully selected not to pander to American stereotypes of the British. Nevertheless Nettleton had peers and contemporaries to share the burden, once Gibson was away from the "top table" party it was clear he was to star on his own. Whilst at times accompanied by various others, including Air Vice Marshall Billy Bishop VC, the WWI fighter ace and first Canadian pilot to receive the VC, in terms of peer pressure Gibson was to be on his own – despite at least one other Dambuster being an American.

What was more unusual about Gibson's trip rather than Nettleton's was that Churchill was crossing the Atlantic for discussions of war-plans. Churchill decided to take both Gibson and Orde Wingate, fresh from his extraordinary exploits in the Far East, as part of his entourage on the trip. Many found Wingate austere but Gibson's personality seemed more congenial to many of the party, not least Churchill's daughter Mary.

Therefore, in August 1943, Gibson went on a goodwill tour of Canada and North America, setting off on the Queen Mary on 5th, initially as part of Churchill's party to have talks with Canadian Prime Minister Mackenzie King and Roosevelt. Officially assigned to Special Duties attached to "Operation Quadrant" Gibson's role, after the international diplomatic formalities, was to go on tour on a PR Offensive to assist Bomber Command, then beginning to feel a personnel crisis about the quality and quantity of recruits.

The Prime Minister's party arrived at Halifax, Nova Scotia, and travelled by train to Quebec arriving there on 10th August. The following day Gibson lunched with the Canadian Prime Minister Mackenzie King – before doing the first of his engagements at a RCAF recruiting centre. It was while the British hero was raising morale and cementing relations that, back in London, the decision was taken to give our Russian Allies the details of Upkeep to cement the relationship with Britain's other ally.

The following day, Gibson's birthday, he faced a large gathering of international journalists from the Free World hosted by the Canadian Air Minister, C.G. Power, at Quebec's Hotel Clarendon, the place where on 17th August 1943 Churchill and Roosevelt stayed for two weeks laying the foundations for the Normandy landings. Gibson always had got on well with "Dominion" airmen, their vitality appealing to his exuberant "can do" nature,

VC MEDAL

The Victoria Cross is Britain's highest award for bravery in combat. Since it was founded in 1856, only 1,356 have been awarded and only three men have ever been awarded a bar. Gibson's VC was gazetted on 28 May, 1943, just 12 days after the raid.

so he could make the correct diplomatic noises with sincerity. The tour started in earnest, the following day even though details are not comprehensively available, but until returning to Prestwick on 1st December 1943 Gibson toured the vastness of Canada and parts of America. In Canada, Gibson mainly served as a recruiting agent and morale builder – an authentic hero with a charming manner. The tours were mainly bases, and training schools, handing out medals and making speeches. There were calls to relatives of the Canadians who had been on the dams' raid with him, a few receptions, a quick dip to New York to appear in a radio play, and not many days off until 4th October.

The tour then shifted into the USA, where Gibson spent more time on the civic audiences, including the Minneapolis Traffic Association which is perhaps a little unexpected, and inevitably press conferences. Gibson also found time to attend a Washington farewell fete for Wing Commander Norton hosted by Air Vice Marshal Walsh RCAF in early October, and to appear on a radio variety show on New York's WJZ, broadcast on 9th October. Gibson received the Legion of Merit at Bolling Field near Washington on 19th October, presented by General Arnold, who had been interested in and supportive of Upkeep and more especially trusted by the British with information, it was an interesting Award to make. By virtue of his rank Gibson may just have qualified for the lowest level of the Award, the Legionnaire; instead Gibson received the Commander level, the second highest level and one where all other, non-American, recipients are at Admiral, or Major-General rank.

The American visit also included a sojourn with Howard Hawks from 2nd to 9th November at his home 1150 Moraga Drive Los Angeles. The Americans had had an idea about making a film of the Raid fairly soon after it happened, the British Embassy in Washington being approached by a New York syndicate King Features, part of the Hearst Corporation. The British welcomed the idea of a film and, when Hawks showed an interest and had secured a budget to make it, Roald Dahl, then a S/Ldr and Assistant Air Attaché at the Washington Embassy, started collaborating with Hawks. The "pitch" that Gibson seems to have dictated, if only because there are transcription errors such as an American would make unfamiliar with Gibson's English accent, bore the date 9th November 1943 and was sent under the auspices of the influential Orsatti Agency. It reads as rip-roaring adventure and bears no sign of external editing although clearly Gibson was given some form of brief given the often gratuitous references to anyone not British – and, incidentally, citing Young as an American. The script reached London by the end of November, Wallis openly critical of the portrayal of scientists in general and himself in particular, Whitworth slightly less critical but not impressed by the misrepresentations of the RAF. The rather Orwellian, to modern ears, Ministry of Information, Press and Censorship Bureau was housed in Senate House within University College London, Arnold's "Godless institution in Gower Street", where Pye had now become the Provost, and it was their job to send British concerns to America. The enthusiasm for an American film therefore cooled, possibly because of newer and more American news, with the project abandoned by February 1944.

On 1st December Gibson departed from Montreal and arrived, via a Liberator, at Prestwick airport – later to also be famous for being the only place Elvis Presley visited in Britain. There was a common theme throughout Gibson's reported comments on both legs of his tour. The war would not be over until the Japanese were beaten, no doubt helping persuade Americans we too were in the war for the long haul, and the quality of the American and Canadian airmen, whether in their own air forces or serving in the RAF The media comment was also uniform, talking of Gibson's youth, modesty, looks and humour as well as his war record – although nuances of detail were often mis-reported. Gibson was noticeably diplomatic talking about American "precision" bombing (which was not very good) to preserve American sensibilities; and, asked about Area Bombing, carefully answered that Bomber Command were taught to believe it would break German morale. This was the period when Churchill was less sure in his support for the concept, and it is noticeable that in his book written just after this trip, Gibson too starts to express doubts about the policy too. Could this weakening of philosophical belief be the real reason behind Harris's much quoted remark about the Americans "spoiling young Gibson"? Was it perhaps not the Americans, but the fact that Gibson had started to lean toward Churchill's shading of opinion?

Gibson returned to his wife, in London, the wife who tour publicity had said worked in a camouflage netting factory. At this time the Gibsons had accommodation at Aberdeen Place, near Lords, and which now has the famous Blue Plaque. Shortly after his return Gibson requested a

US LEGION OF MERIT

In December 1943 Gibson was awarded the Legion of Merit (Commander) by US President Franklin D. Roosevelt. The award recognises exceptional instances of military leadership and, unusually for an American medal, is worn on a ribbon around the neck.

return to Operations, instead obtaining a month's leave for being "Non-operational sick".

Transferred, on 3rd January 1944, to the Air Ministry Directorate – Prevention of Accidents, after returning to England it seems that in reality the RAF wanted Gibson to write his book. Gibson duly wrote "Enemy Coast Ahead", which was published posthumously, and reprinted regularly, is now also available in an uncensored version. There have been suggestions that Gibson did not write the book and it was a production by Sqn Ldr Roald Dahl, but those who knew Gibson say it is very much in his breezy style and that "Chiefy" Powell from No.617 Squadron assisted in the actual production.

The future career path for Gibson was not certain - what role was there for someone who was now too much of a legend to do what had made him a legend, but who had so much operational experience? Churchill had an idea and was not alone in looking to the resumption of political dissent after the War. Impressed by Gibson, and seeking what we would now call "bright young men" Gibson's name came up when the Conservative Member of Parliament for Macclesfield, Willard Garfield Weston, made clear he wanted to retire to concentrate on his extensive business interests – in those days that was not a euphemism. The Conservative "magic circle" worked its way and Gibson "evolved" and "emerged" as a man with an interest in Macclesfield and politics. Published after Gibson's death Eve wrote about his reasons for wishing to be an MP.:

"The answer is simple. What this country needs is young men like myself.

Young men who have seen the destruction of cities which will have to be rebuilt. And for what purpose? Another war in twenty years time? No Eve. The world's been run by politicians and industrialists since the first world war, greedy men, men too old to fight. But they didn't mind sending thousands like me to our deaths. There must never be another war because the next one will be even worse. It'll be the end of all time. I hope you won't be alive to see it"

Later in February, Gibson made his appearance on Desert Island Discs with the "Professor of Polite Interest, Roy Plomley" Gibson's choices were:-

Richard Addinsell - Warsaw Concerto

Jack Hylton's Orchestra - Where or When (from Babes In Arms)

Johann Strauss II - A Thousand and One Nights Waltz

Richard Wagner - The Flying Dutchman

Bing Crosby - If I Had My Way

Fred Waring & His Pennsylvanians - The Marines Hymn.

The Central Band of The Royal Air Force - Royal Air Force March Past

Richard Wagner - Ride of the Valkyries (from Die Walküre)

Perhaps the most surprising matter of these choices, apart from there being no censorship about the two tunes by Hitler's favourite composer and one of them in a version by the Berlin State Opera Orchestra, was indeed the eighth choice. Before Coppola had the idea in "Apocalypse Now" Gibson opined, "there were quite a lot of contestants for the last place. Wagner won in the end. I want "The Ride of the Valkeries". It's exciting, it's grandiose, it's – rather terrible. It reminds me of a bombing raid. Though I don't say it's like one".

As ever in the Armed Services, when uncertain what to do with operational men who, for whatever reason, have a less clear operational career path – staff work becomes the solution, although it was not what Gibson sought. On 13th March 1944, Gibson joined the prestigious RAF Staff College, then at Bulstrode Park, entering the 28th Group Course.

Despite selection for the Staff College, the RAF also gave Gibson permission to be a Prospective Parliamentary Candidate – and time to go to a selection meeting in Macclesfield on 25th March. Perhaps the most interesting candidate Gibson beat for selection in that Conservative selection meeting was Air Vice Marshal Don "Pathfinder" Bennett – even more curious when it is recalled Bennett was elected in 1945 as a Liberal!

The first anniversary of the Dambuster Raid was a great cause for a party at No.617 Squadron. Naturally, Gibson was invited but Staff College duties prevented him attending the Officers Party. The language in the telegram, from Gerrards Cross immediately adjacent to Bulstrode Park, expresses Gibson's views of Staff College life rather well, "Awfully sorry unable to come because of exercise 'Bumph', have a terrific party best to Cheshire and all the boys = Guy Gibson". Wing Commander Leonard Cheshire was, by this date, commander of the squadron.

The RAF's most decorated officer would no doubt have had a view about the entry in the 55 Base ORB for 19th May 1944, "The following Directing staff and students of RAF Staff College visited East Kirkby for one night in order to attend briefing and Flight Planning. W/C Craven DFC, W/C Baird AFC, S/L Bryant Fenn DFC , Major Gardner, W/C Gibson VC DSO DFC, S/Ldr Richardson DFC, W/C Robinson. The object of the visit was to give students an insight into the workings of a typical night Bombing Station." Just over a year after the Dams raid, which, however atypical, was only possible because of people who had learned their jobs doing typical missions, Gibson was back on a station to see how it worked!

However, being on a trip to Lincolnshire, meant Gibson could accept the invitation to the all ranks No.617 Squadron dance on 19th May. The in-house 54-Base magazine, "The Gen" sums up the evening and encompasses Gibson's status at the time. After commenting there were huge cheers when Gibson and Cheshire walked in together, "From then on both he and Wing Commander Cheshire were besieged by swarms of the erks, and after much persuasion, both agreed to cut a birthday cake (Complete with all the trimmings). This having been done to the accompaniment of almost deafening cheers, they were both hoisted onto the table and ordered to make speeches"

"W/Cdr Cheshire opened by paying warm tribute to W/Cdr Gibson and to all members of the Squadron past and present, who took part in that memorable raid. He then called upon W/Cdr Gibson, whose speech consisted of one word 'Thanks'. This did not satisfy the audience who hoisted him up again, unfortunately to the detriment of his best blue, as he was unceremoniously deposited in the middle of the birthday cake. He did, however, make a short speech, in which he expressed his pleasure at being back with the Squadron again, if only for an evening."

Somehow the picture of a Luftwaffe hero being so retiring and then pressed into action by his juniors does not seem likely.

The Staff College Course finished at the end of May and Gibson went on holiday with Eve, in North Wales, for a week, during which news came of Operation Overlord.

Gibson's log-book on his return from Canada is stark in its simplicity – against January, February, and March appears the solitary word "nil". A 3-hour flight in an Airspeed Oxford transport from Turnhouse to Woodhouse

LOCKHEED LIGHTNING

The unusual Lockheed P-38 Lightning was flown by Gibson several times, though he piloted it on only one raid over enemy territory. The aircraft was designed to be a long-range escort fighter, but pilots found it too stable to be effective in a dog fight so it was often used for ground attack or reconnaissance purposes

and return on 30th April and again in May "nil". Gibson, who had joined the RAF solely to fly so he could be a test pilot, was in neither the war nor even flying. Because the war was finally turning in the Allies favour, and Gibson felt he was too inactive, he went to see Harris and within days that equally decisive commander had Gibson transferred closer to the action. Finally, Gibson returned to 5 Group taking up the role of operations officer at 55 Base in East Kirkby.

During WW2, the expansion of Bomber Command was such that there were insufficient senior officers with the relevant experience to command all the new stations and the R.A.F introduced the Base System. Introduced in March 1943, the intention behind the Base System was to simplify the command structure and improve operational logistics. Normally commanded by an Air Commodore and serving as an intermediate level of command between Group HQs and the RAF Station a Base normally grouped two 'satellite' airfields to a main airfield thereby bringing several small bases under one station commander and centralising the administration and maintenance on one newer and larger station.

East Kirkby had opened on 15th April 1944 authorised by a letter from Bomber Command of 22nd April 1944 and at the time Gibson, arrived 12th June 1944, it had 57 Squadron and 630 Squadron based there. At the time of Gibson's arrival East Kirkby had responsibility for Spilsby and, shortly after his arrival from July 1944 took responsibility for Strubby the most easterly bomber base but which was primarily used operationally by Coastal Command.

Gibson did not fly again officially until 28th June when he did a return flight to Spilsby in an Oxford, but on 5th July Gibson, for the first time in eight months, went up in a Lancaster of 57 Squadron for some local flying.

Former Dambuster colleague Mick Martin came to visit Gibson on 10th July. Now a Squadron Leader, Martin was flying the Mosquito with 515 Squadron, which undertook night intruder missions in support of other Bomber Command raids. Gibson had his first flight in "the wooden wonder" engaging in local flying, his logbook clearly showing Martin as the main pilot. Reportedly, Martin states they discussed Gibson's political career amongst other matters and it may well have solidified Gibson's thoughts on his future.

It was in July that Gibson decided his political career was not for him. By now based at East Kirkby Gibson wrote on 5th July that he was "fully determined to fight the Japs after this war" and that "the very fact that I have been interested in Politics does not seem to have enhanced my service career, and I cannot bring myself to make Political Speeches which might do even further harm". Following a brief hospitalisation with a type of sinusitis, Gibson redeveloped his theme, that he was perhaps a little young and the conflict between trying to fight the enemy and making speeches was too great. He confirmed he was withdrawing from the candidature for Macclesfield. The resignation was handled and completed by 14th August.

On 19th July Gibson became operational again when he flew on an operation to Creil near Paris. In a Lancaster, in daylight operations and encountering moderate flak Gibson recorded "Successful. Aiming Point. Mod flak" in his log-book. The picture posted in his log-book showed Gibson was still operationally competent.

The next flight was a week later doing smoke trials, again in a Lancaster, on 26th July

Posted at the beginning of August 1944 to be the Base Air Staff Officer (BASO) at No.54 Base, formed in August 1943 at Coningsby, Gibson returned to the airfield of his first command. The Base ORB recorded on 2nd August that Gibson was, "Posted from 55 Base for Operational Duties. W/Cdr Post. Reported 4.8.44".

Coningsby was altogether a more significant posting, a Base which had Woodhall Spa, where No.617 Squadron was rostered; and Metheringham, where No.106 Squadron, Gibson's other command, was located as part of the confederation. To complete the sense of circles closing Gibson's first operational posting, No.83 Squadron, were now at Coningsby.

Gibson stepped up his flying, logging time on an Oxford flying around the local area and going to the different airfields introducing himself. Time was also found to try out a Lockheed Lightning, an unusual American long-range fighter with twin fuselage. Gibson then flew a Lightning on a mission to Deelen airfield in Holland on 16th/17th August, although Gibson's log says 18th . Deelen airfield was a Luftwaffe base close to Arnheim, the battle for which would start on 17th September, and where military necessity meant denying the Germans the use of the airfield. It seems unlikely Gibson was engaged in overt hostility since he was in a Lightning, and this was a minor raid, but it was still operational and "combat orientation" since "gardening" was now seldom an option.

Gibson's current operational status meant the prohibition on wives he had embraced, with some willingness, when he commanded No.106 Squadron was less of a consideration, and so he was able to have Eve nearby again. Gibson secured lodgings in Skegness and they had a meal on Guy's birthday, seemingly the last time they would see each other.

The suggestion of combat orientation is reinforced reading that Gibson's log-book records him, on 22nd August, again flying a Lightning when he followed a Bomber Stream to Fecamp, a French fishing port halfway from Dieppe to Le Havre. The clear implication, given the complete military blandness of Fecamp was that the Bombers were going on but Gibson was obeying instructions not to stray too far into Germany. The position of Base Officers was unusual in that, theoretically no longer operational, their rank meant they could choose to go as passenger or even operationally periodically.

DE HAVILLAND MOSQUITO
Intended to be used as a high-speed, precision bomber, the Mosquito proved to be one of the most versatile aircraft of the war. Gibson was flying a Mosquito in his role as a master bomber when he was killed.

Some Base Officers who went on missions had lost their lives, and whilst guidelines existed, there seems little doubt that a national hero and international name like Gibson would have stricter orders leaving little room for interpretation.

Gibson's next flights were internal, generally around the stations within his Base, using the Oxford. Gibson's second recorded flight in a Mosquito was on 31st August spending over an hour with it on local flights. Although accompanied by a fellow Wing Commander, this time Gibson was the first pilot. The following day Gibson, and a junior officer as second pilot, took off on a 5-hour flight. The log-book records "To Scatsta–Wick then all points north". Wick, is the most northerly airport in mainland Britain, and Scatsta, also known as Scatsa, on the Shetland Isles is the most northerly airfield in the British Isles. Denied the chance to practice endurance flights over the steadily crumbling Fortress Europe the supposition Gibson was orientating himself to become "match tough" on a new aeroplane Martin had enthused him with seems a sustainable point of view.

The draft of "Enemy Coast Ahead" came back at this point – the PR section of the Air Ministry had already used part of it, and the usual fine-tuning took place. The censors argued about some of the operational details, and the publisher had yet to exercise his power to exorcise; however to all intents and purposes the work was finished as far as Gibson was concerned.

The ORB for Station Headquarters at Woodhall Spa records on 3rd September 1944 that Sir Archibald Sinclair visited No.54 Base. Arriving at Coningsby around 10:45 the log records he was welcomed by the Base Commander and other dignitaries including "the Base Air Staff Officer (Wing Commander G.P. Gibson, V.C., D.S.O., D.F.C.". This is the last record of Gibson, whilst alive, in an ORB.

Gibson made two more local flights, in an Oxford and a Mosquito, in the latter Gibson again flew with W/Cdr Woodroffe, one of the controllers from the Base. Woodroffe then accompanied Gibson to Le Havre where filming was undertaken. Le Havre was being heavily bombed in support of the two British Divisions attacking it, and the figures show the air-superiority Bomber Command had achieved against the crumbling Reich. Commencing on 5th September and including the raid Gibson accompanied on the 10th, weather allowed four days to successful bomb Le Havre: which 1793 aircraft did for a loss, in total, of two aircraft.

A few domestic flights as a passenger in a Lancaster, and a flight in an Oxford filming a Lancaster fill up Gibson's log-book. The final entry records a visit to Langford Lodge, a USAAF aircraft depot near Belfast mainly used to process aircraft on their way to active service in the British, mainland Europe, North African, and Mediterranean war zones.

When not on operational duties Gibson was still on the usual "hearts and minds" duties of senior servicemen. Brief remarks to Scouts (available on "YouTube"), and presenting prizes on school sports day at De Aston Grammar, Market Rasen not long before he was killed.

Gibson's last raid was on Mönchengladbach and Rheydt. Rheydt is a suburb of Monchengladbach now but there is a certain irony that Gibson, with operational hours severely curtailed to deny the Germans a propaganda coup, should die attacking the birth-place of the Reich's Minister for Propaganda. Some circumstances of Gibson's death remain unclear, but not all.

The Bomber Command Night Raid Report (No.719) Narrative of Attack baldly sums up the mission, "The first AP was most accurately marked and bombed; but on the second AP, the TI of the Controller (who failed to return) are thought to have hung up, and some early crews attacked the third AP. Eventually, however, the second AP was properly marked, and the bombing appeared good. Smoke obscured ground detail during the later stages of the attack on the third AP and crews were told to concentrate on the fires". Such is the language of officialdom when a hero does not return!

It is clear Gibson flew a Canadian built Mosquito XX, KB267, part of No.627 Squadron and he was flying with the Base Navigation Officer F/Lt James Warwick who had been made-up to be Acting S/Ldr to reflect the rank the post required. Warwick had completed two tours, latterly on Lancasters, and earned a DFC in the process. Uncertainty then commences around even which airfield Gibson took off from! Generally, the SOP (Standard Operating Practice) was that Controllers usually took off from Coningsby. That there were no serviceable Mosquitoes and Gibson loaned one from Woodhall Spa, part of the Base confederation and less than five miles away is also generally accepted. However there is, currently no documentary evidence where Gibson took off from to go on the mission, each ORB being silent on the topic.

The raid on Mönchengladbach and Rheydt itself was unusual. Bomber Command had traditionally worked to a plan where there was one aiming point per target. However, there were times when there could be multiple targets the Base ORB writing of the growing trend that marking and bombing techniques had, "been developed even further, so much so that several targets are now being attacked on the same night by separate Squadrons within a Base." On this night the plan was to bomb three separate aiming points within the target area.

The Woodhall Spa Summary of Operations for the Night of 19th/20th September 1944 is quite clear. Commenting on the Red Marking Point it records that the "Flares went down at 2133/4 and were slightly too N and E of the M.P." (Marking Point) whereupon the Report continues that the controller had identified target "and was making a run, but his T.I.'s apparently failed to release and he called upon red markers to carry out the marking". (T.I. meaning Target Indicators). Two Mosquitoes were unable to identify correctly the target and a third was not in a correct position to make a successful run. Gibson then called on the Red Force to attack the green Marking Point but one of the Mosquitoes was now in a position to deliver accurately on the red aiming point. Bombers that had not diverted on to another target in the mission then followed up with accurate bombing.

Gibson's last remarks heard over the air are, as is the way of things, the subject of differing emphasis in the recall of different people. The common agreement seems to be that Gibson praised the crews and sent them home with the variations being around whether they were to get tea or beer and whether or not it was "head off" or "bugger off".

Again accounts seem to agree that the last the RAF saw of Gibson was him circling the target at 2,000 feet. It was usual for controllers to observe the raid results, Gibson often doing so even before the concept of the Master Bomber he had pioneered at the Dams, and indeed he had done it at the Dams. With a stated intent to leave Europe flying fast and low, which again casts doubt on the claims of being shot down by a Lancaster gunner, Gibson eventually headed home and his aircraft was seen by contemporary Dutch witnesses who came forward at the time.

Gibson crashed when homebound near Steenbergen-en-Kruisland, some 8 miles north of Bergen-op-Zoom, Noord-Brabant, Holland. At approximately 22.30, on 18th September, one year and three days after his 617 crew were recorded as missing, Gibson's Mosquito crashed on farmland near Steenbergen and exploded. Morris, in his book, quotes eye-witnesses who saw the Mosquito on fire, none of whom make mention of any other aircraft in the vicinity. Cutler, most recently cited in "Britain at War" Magazine (October 2011), has the taped recollection of an eye-witness who said he shot him down mistaking the Mosquito for a Junkers Ju88. Some eye-witness somewhere must be mistaken! However the fact remains that Gibson had, for the second time in his life crashed and this time, the man who had looked death in the face so often he could almost call him a friend had finally crossed over. The last irony of Gibson's life was he died flying an aircraft manufactured by a company owned by Geoffrey de Havilland, who had been educated at his own school, St Edward's.

Gibson was buried at the small Catholic cemetery at Steenbergen, Bergen op zoom, in Holland the Germans not aware who was being buried in what was, originally, a single grave until the Dutch realised who it was and could admit it once the Germans had gone. It is not much to the RAF's credit that it was largely neglected and it was largely through the efforts of members of the former Dutch resistance most especially, Jan van den Driesschen in 1965, that the Grave was tidied up. In this country Gibson is commemorated on Penarth (Glamorgan) War Memorial, Gibson left no Will his wealth at death being recorded as £2925 7s. 2d. and administration granted on 7th July 1945. Gibson's father waived his share of the estate in favour of Guy's widow.

Back in England the Base Commander in his remarks recorded, "The Base and the RAF as a whole suffered a heavy loss when W/Cdr Gibson, VC, DSO, DFC, failed to return from the attack on Mönchengladbach. He was controlling the operation and was last heard of circling the target at 2,000 feet in order to assess results. W/Cdr Gibson came to the Base as BASO, in August and during his short stay with us had impressed us all with his keenness, efficiency and charming personality. It was typical of him to insist on undertaking the operation in question, although this was not strictly part of his duties as a Staff Officer. We earnestly hope to hear good news of him and his navigator shortly."

Although by now there was an awareness Gibson was dead it had still not been officially announced which may explain why the ORB for 54 Base reported Gibson very much in the present tense on 11th October 1944. The Base Commander, was about to go to India, and amongst the usual farewell speech contents "special thanks were given to the Squadrons for their operational record and to the Squadron Commanders" that are then listed chronologically by squadron with no mention of "the late" before Gibson's name.

The delays continued until Gibson was officially announced "Missing" on 29th November, 25 days after the liberation of Steenbergen.

Indeed the official announcement of the death of Wing Commander Guy Gibson, VC, DSO★ DFC★ would not be made until 8th January 1945. Characteristically Churchill wrote to Gibson's widow before the official announcement. The West Briton newspaper duly reported on Gibson under the title "Dam Buster's body found"

RAF GRAVES OF GIBSON AND WARWICK
Gibson and his co-pilot Squadron Leader Jim Warwick DFC were killed when their Mosquito crashed near Steenbergen in the Netherlands. The two men are buried side by side in the village churchyard.

The Legacy

Arguably, part of the definition of a hero is if they, or their deeds, are remembered after their death. However, memory and awareness of Gibson seems to be consistent over the decades, to some extent he is now more talked about than other heroes of RAF Bomber Command. What follows is by no means comprehensive or all-inclusive, but it does represent a broad continuum in a theme. The theme of not forgetting, perhaps best summed up in the words of Laurence Binyon's best-known poem For The Fallen (1914), most notably the celebrated fourth stanza:

"They shall not grow old as we that are left grow old:
Age shall not weary them, nor the years condemn.
At the going down of the sun and in the morning,
We will remember them."

A huge step towards a legacy came with the publication of Gibson's own book first published as a book in 1946, after serialisation in "The Sunday Express" during the winter of 1944-45, almost continuously in print since and followed up by an uncensored account released in 2003. The book was followed by Paul Brickhill's "The Dam Busters" in 1954 also almost continuously in print since and both books helped shape the 1955

RAF CHURCH AT ST CLEMENT DANES
On 10 May 1941 a Luftwaffe raid gutted the church of St Clement Danes in the City of London. The church was rebuilt by public subscription to act as the main church of the RAF. An inscription over the door reads "Built by Christopher Wren 1682. Destroyed by the thunderbolts of air warfare 1941. Restored by the Royal Air Force 1958."

British made "The Dam Busters" starring Richard Todd and Michael Redgrave - itself a regular staple of TV and even featured in a recent "Summer of British Film".

The RAF Church at St Clement Danes has, amongst all other recipients of the VC, Gibson's name on a plaque near the altar and, 25 years after the raid, survivors held a thanksgiving at St Clements. Dambuster survivors regularly make clear they do not regard any event as a celebration, survivors commenting they cannot celebrate when so many friends were lost and preferring the word "commemoration". The RAF also named a VC10 after Gibson and produced the ephemera to match as well.

The Dutch, with a long history of admiration for the work of the RAF have two streets named after both Gibson and Warwick in Steenbergen, and marked them with a brick mosaic of the Union Flag at the intersection.

There was a reunion in Canada in 1972 and in 1976 a tour in Holland including Gibson's grave and a Lancaster fly-past over that. In 1977 over 5000 people watched the Lancaster fly over Derwent Water while six survivors of the raid stood on the wall of the dam. Later, in 1977, on Sir Barnes Wallis' 90th birthday there was a commemoration at Thatcher's hotel in East Horsley. In September 1979, Dutch resistance fighters give the R.A.F museum at Hendon a plaque, and during the decade Gibson also saw that ultimate accolade in Britain – a flower named after him. In this horticultural case, a Dahlia commemorated Gibson and there is also a Dahlia named Inca Dambuster.

In January 1981 Gibson's gold cigarette case, presented to him by Vickers, was sold at auction. Inscribed, "ED932-G GPG May 17th 1943 Nigger Dinghy" it was purchased for £4,600. The Lincoln Chronicle reported in January 1981 Sothebys had sold the case to a Doncaster businessman who had outbid several of Gibson's contemporaries. Reflecting the value of the legend far more than the value of a gold case itself, it was sold for six times the estimate.

In the nineteen-nineties, there fell the 50th anniversary of the dam raid. The RAF co-operated with the B.B.C.'s "Songs of Praise" for a big event ultimately shown in many parts of the world and the following year Gibson remained unforgotten by a newer generation of the RAF when two Tornadoes flew over his grave on 19th Sept 1994.

Consideration of the legacy in the current century in some ways takes it back to the 1950's by referencing Peter Jackson's much talked of remake of "The Dam Busters". In 2004 Mel Gibson had dropped the rights to a remake of Anderson's film and subsequently Sir David Frost purchased the rights from the Brickhill family in 2005. Stephen Fry is writing the script of the film, famously agonising over the name of poor "Nigger", who was already renamed "Trigger" in an American edition of the original British classic. Apparently "Nigger" is now to be known as "Digger".

On 16th May 2008, the 65th anniversary, a commemoration was again held at Derwent Reservoir, including a fly-past by a Lancaster and which was attended by Les Munro, the last pilot from the original raid still living, and Richard Todd as well as Mary Stopes-Roe, the daughter of Sir Barnes Wallis who by then was also dead.

In 2010 Gibson was commemorated at Penarth by the RAFA and plans for a newer and bigger memorial in Porthleven were announced.

WOODHALL SPA MEMORIAL
Close to the crossroads in the centre of the Lincolnshire village of Woodhall Spa stands this memorial to the men who died serving in No.617 Squadron. The memorial takes the form of a dam with water gushing through a breach.

115

THE FOCKE WULFE FW190

The Focke Wulfe FW190 was arguably the best
German fighter of the war. Several FW190
nightfighters were in the air on the night that
Gibson died and one of them may have been
involved in his death.

The value of a Gibson/Dambuster connection continues when even
an AEC petrol tanker used by the squadron in World War II was sold
for £17,500 at auction. Built in 1943, and sent to Scampton where it
served with Bomber Command until 1949, it was not even clear it had
arrived in time for the raid on the dams but the squadron connection was
enough and a lorry thought to be only worth about £2,000 went for a
considerable premium.

Bringing matters right up to date we have, literally as of writing this part
of the book in 2011, the latest in the theorising of Gibson's death. "Britain
At War" magazine (October 2011) carries an article in which James Cutler,
researching for the long saga about the projected remake of the Dambusters,
theorises that Gibson was downed by a Sergeant Bernard McCormack, a
mid–upper gunner in a Lancaster, who fired 600 rounds. This has provoked
widespread media interest and provoked lively internet discussion. Clearly
McCormack believed he had shot down Gibson, although as so often these
matters emerge after the person involved is no longer available to be asked
to revisit their, almost certainly, painful memories. McCormack died in 1992
but his wife gave Cutler a tape of his recollection as part of Cutler's research.

Afterword

I have written this book like an historian should. I have tried to stick to ascertainable facts, and avoid speculation, with little interpolation of myself into the book being ever mindful of Professor E.H. Carr's injunction that it is not the role of the historian to scurry around granting absolution here and condemnation there. I ask indulgence to discuss my thoughts on what heroism is and why Guy was a hero. It may also be timely, in view of the most recent public interest, to touch on the death of a hero.

Cutler relies on a report in the National Archives by the crew of the Lancaster describing the incident. Declaring himself "satisfied 100 percent" that Guy Gibson was killed by friendly fire and 99.9 percent sure Gibson was shot down by McCormack's Lancaster, Cutler thereby minimises the report that "Gibson's" (unarmed) Mosquito fired back. Furthermore believing the absence of German records of a Junkers Ju88 being near Steenbergen is positive evidence there were no German aircraft in the area, is to rely on a stereotype about German record keeping and a belief that records are sacrosanct when, my own researches would suggest, they are all too often incomplete or contradictory and not immune from error. Indeed Cutler makes the very point about contradictory British records himself in the article.

It also begs the question why, when Gibson had professed he was going to fly out from Europe at low level - an action he was urged against - McCormack's Lancaster was flying at low level, or conversely why Gibson was flying at high altitude in the standard Lancaster stream's height of around 10,000 feet. Hypothesising Gibson was lost, when accompanied by the Base Navigation Officer, seems unlikely looking at his route but, even if true, it requires a major leap of faith to think that all Gibson could think of to find his way home was to creep up on a Lancaster, on its most heavily defended spot.

If we examine the idea that the rear-gunner was not active in this exchange we have a twin-gunned upper turret with a Browning .303 discharging 1,150

117

bullets a minute. Two guns would therefore discharge 2300 a minute (incidentally the cone of fire was around 200 feet so this would be a lucky long-range shot or if the aircraft was closing with lights on as claimed then the gunners must have been slow to spot it and identify it) which is 38 rounds a second. To fire 600 rounds would therefore take fifteen seconds which is a very long burst indeed – and if so the damage must have been slight since the witnesses record the Mosquito, the only aircraft they heard, circling for a while with a spluttering engine.

Exploring German records is mentioned in the Cutler article but what is not mentioned is another interesting claim I picked up, and one which also helps demonstrate the problems of records. There was a claim that Gibson was shot down by German ace Kurt Welter – on the grounds that he claimed a mosquito that night, only Gibson's mosquito was lost that night q.e.d Welter shot down Gibson – despite nobody hearing gunfire or another engine. Modern research suggests a degree of inflation in Welter's claims but also that he was flying over North Wittenberg over 200 miles away when he shot down a Mosquito some thirty-five minutes after Gibson had crashed. Either there was a second mosquito lost, or the records of where Welter was are wrong, or German records are as fallible as British ones.

The other common-place theory, often presented as an internet fact, is that Gibson ran out of fuel and this has been "proven" by finding the fuel tank selector. The Dutch, who excavated Gibson's Mosquito, did not find anything like a switch – which would make sense as the "wooden wonder" was known to burn fiercely – and on top of that natural tendency to burn, it is not wholly clear Gibson had managed to release his marker bomb, the probability being he had not, given the discovery of a burnt out TI flare at the site. It is likely that the Mosquito would already have switched fuel tanks before it reached Mönchengladbach. Because the outer fuel tanks in a Mosquito had a capacity which allowed some 250 miles, and were intended to be used first, with Rheydt being 300 miles away, it seems likely the tanks would have been switched over by the time Gibson reached the target. In any event Gibson himself wrote, "The most important thing of all is this cockpit drill business, when flying modern aircraft. All it means is getting to know the position of every tap so that you can fly the aircraft without having to look down for the controls. All movements have to be made automatically as one does when driving a car. When flying a big bomber on a misty night, that split second when the pilot might turn his head away from the instruments might mean the difference between life and death". It seems inconceivable that Gibson would not stick to this advice, especially knowing he was going to be flying low.

I certainly reject the idea that Gibson was inexperienced on the aircraft, and unfamiliar with the master bomber concept. Briefed by Mick Martin, and going up with him it is inconceivable that two adventurous pilots would fly sedate "circuit and bumps". The 900 mile round-trip to the north of Scotland involved the need for airborne fuel-tank switchover, in most circumstances a job for the navigator, on both legs of the journey and a flight of such length, and involving landing at difficult airfields, shows Gibson indeed did have flight familiarisation. In fact, as a combat veteran, Gibson had 7 ½ hours practice on a Manchester before his first operation, and had done 9 ½ as First Pilot on the Mosquito before his first operation on one of those but pundits do not suggest an unfamiliarity with the Manchester! In his early familiarisation, flights on the Mosquito Gibson purposefully flew with a controller from the Base, and from this we could draw the conclusion that he received the necessary operational familiarisation. Gibson had flown in a Mosquito with Mick Martin, a friend, and discovering what the aircraft could do had been enthused by that. Familiarisation exercises with a base controller, followed by a five-hour familiarisation flight with a junior officer, another local flight with the same base controller, an operation over enemy territory with the same base controller are all suggestive of a man who knew what he wanted to do next in the RAF.

Dutch eye-witnesses at the time, and they lived long enough to be interviewed, reported the engine spluttering. The Merlin was a generally reliable power-plant but no engine is infallible, and if we accept the contemporary statements of eye witnesses, recalled at the time, that the engine was sputtering so fuel supply may well have been the problem. However it does not follow that fuel starvation is simply a result of a switch, it is maybe more likely that a simple mechanical failure ended Gibson's life - his luck just ran out as so many others' had and would. The only truth about why Gibson died is that we do not know and almost certainly never will. However, in terms of myths and mythologising the burning hero warrior ascending in a chariot of fire, if there must be an end, is fitting. However what is the "hero concept" and is it truly applicable?

Heroes are not necessarily as modern culture has them. The word is rapidly becoming debased following the American custom of now referring to anyone who serves in the military routinely as "hero". Once "Hero" meant someone distinguished by extraordinary deeds, often a warrior – a nod to the classical Greek meaning of superhuman strength or feats endowed on a mortal by the Gods. To some extent we have returned to that classical meaning of "hero" as a larger than life representation, in part as influenced by Hollywood, through some sort of gung-ho John Wayne, or cavalierly insouciant Errol Flynn. I would not criticise that, I enjoy the movies of both and have done all my life – but that is not to say I accept the definition of heroism portrayed there.

Real heroism is often quieter, more deliberative and more introspective. It is often about fighting the fear within as much as the enemy. Even in his lifetime people attempted to portray Gibson as heroic and fearless when he, as he said frequently, was not – Gibson quoted Humphreys writing just before dispersal on the Dams Raid, "The Wing Commander turned up in his car prompt to time with crew. How they all got into that car beats me. He looked fit and well and quite unperturbed [This was a complete lie. – G.G.]". That in many ways is true heroism, to overcome doubts and fears and, to do that is as much a measure of a man for, as Shakespeare had it in "Measure for Measure" "Our doubts are traitors, And make us lose the good we oft might win, By fearing to attempt". Well Gibson certainly passed that test the test to be able to go out there and "do your job".

Gibson nowadays tends to be portrayed as a "martinet" or "controversial", and the adjective "egotistical" is bandied around, whilst the internet abounds with stories of someone who knew somebody (now dead and therefore unable to be checked with) who just heard this or that – yet the facts are remarkably thin on the ground. Sometimes the facts bear little scrutiny, as in the story Morris cites in his book – so what if you buy a round of cigarettes and then put the empty box on the fire?! Yet careless repetition of words will simply not do, bandied around as if the mere use of them, repeated with no analysis of why they were ever used and thoughtlessly repeated, is an argument or an insult itself. Egotists are "all about themselves" but we have seen Gibson avoided speeches unless pressed to do them, and rarely talked about himself – for Gibson it was about deeds and actions; and if a confidence in his own abilities meant he wanted things done a particular way, it was experience talking and not egotism.

Egotism may arguably derive from two sources, a worldview intellectually built around oneself, or subconscious self-absorption and self-love. Those who suggest Gibson was not a deep-thinker in some ways make the point for us – it is an act of conscious thought to assume one is at the heart of the universe, that an intellectual structure can be built around oneself – which negates that form of egotism. There is too much evidence that Gibson enjoyed parties and could form intimacies with aircrews, and dominion personnel to be entirely in the thrall of subconscious self-absorption and self-love. Put simply Gibson was the embodiment of the "actions speak louder than words" school of Englishness: he knew he was good, the facts spoke for that. Whether he knew why he was good is another matter. Probably, lacking cerebral introspection and contemplation, Gibson didn't know why he was good – what he knew was he tried hard, this was a recurrent theme in many remarks he made about himself and as a result of that self-discipline over his actions felt that others should also apply themselves. The decision about whether the triumph of application was to try and help people survive or just petty power-plays is pure speculation and it is time more writers admitted that was what they were doing.

So what was it that made Guy Gibson such a pre-eminent bomber pilot, "chevalier sans peur et sans raproche" as Anthony Verrier, no supporter of the Dams Strategy, wrote? Was he the best pilot in the RAF? Gibson thought Hopgood a better pilot than him in No.617 Squadron, and never made a claim to be the best – and there are those who would say Mick Martin was a more accomplished flyer. Gibson was not the only hero in the War, he was not the only multiple medal winner, nor the first to get a VC, nor the only one to write his memoirs. Operational longevity plays a part, Gibson certainly bucked the odds for a long time and the shifting between Commands was far from normal, but ultimately I think Gibson's talent was what was commented on at school and what meant he caught the eye of Harris: determination. The boy that put on an heroic innings at a cricket match, who tried to fit in, was the same man who became a "hard charger" determined to succeed at his job. Gibson was able to be steadfast, to see a job through, and to drive himself to do it. Within Gibson was a technical ability and competence – shown by how many aircraft of differing types he flew and never rated less than "above average" in both Fighters and Bombers.

However above all was his ability to work out a solution, to adapt to new ways whilst aware he needed other people for areas he had either no aptitude for or no interest. Gibson was a "can do" man, a man of action, a man of deeds, at ease with events.

Because Gibson was a less cerebral commander than others, Cheshire for example, there has emerged a tendency to compare and contrast the two, portraying Gibson as a "hearty" to Cheshire's "sensitive". Well comparisons are odious, and neither man was, nor made claim to be, what many portrayed them as. Indeed, as Shannon remarked, Cheshire could appear "cold and aloof" and it certainly was not Gibson who conceived the idea of an early morning run for the whole Squadron on New Year's Day! Both were great Bomber commanders, neither was perfect, and who of us are? For it is one of the peculiarities of life that, as imperfect human beings ourselves, we award a persona to people we have not met and then award that persona with a perfection we know that is not in ourselves. Then, when we find the heroes are not the "graven idols" we thought they were the denigration begins. Gibson died, Cheshire lived to become a member of CND and founded his famous homes for the disabled. Gibson died, and is fixed in time as the "hearty" that never grew old – literally.

Yet the attempts to portray Gibson as a gung-ho hearty are ultimately flawed. My father, himself a pilot of bombers, when I began to fly reminded me of the old adage: "There are old pilots, there are bold pilots; but there are no old and bold pilots". Gibson knew what he was doing and we have no higher authority about that than Cochrane – himself by nature far from a hearty. It was Cochrane who wrote of Gibson, "Thus ended a career which has few equals in the history of air warfare – a career of action, of which the mainspring was a wholly phenomenal faith. Given this faith, all things were possible, for if the devil ever temptingly suggested that a project was beyond him, he would unceremoniously order him where he belonged. In this attitude, there was nothing that was foolhardy, for every action which he took was planned in detail and he knew precisely what he would do in every emergency. Throughout he had the loyal support of all who flew with him." Gibson was a hard-charger, he was not a gung-ho fool.

When I was young living in Germany, my Dutch nanny (the exchange rate was superb back then) told me how the exploits of the RAF were mentioned by her parents and how the RAF kept hopes alive, to her to be associated with the RAF was a pleasure, which I hope I didn't ruin! When I was a bit older I read a tatty old copy of "Enemy Coast Ahead" I found at my Grandfather's and was thrilled by the exploits and wanted to join the RAF whilst secretly not convinced I was all that brave. By the time I was a rebellious teen Gibson was still a talisman, I wrote to "The Times" and they sent me a copy of his obituary for a school project. Who knows what the chord was that struck me then and made him a hero to me? Is it necessary to intellectualise everything?

In any event, Guy Gibson was a boyhood hero of mine – that makes him a hero of the RAF to me, I hope it does for you too.

Acknowledgments

I t has been a great pleasure to write this, and if it seems like a "lovvie" speech from the Oscars well feel free to read the book! However this is my first book – it may even be my last – so there are a lot of acknowledgements needed. There is no conscious order to these, every piece of help has been valued and appreciated – as Marvel said "no man is an island, centre unto himself".

I found a lot of information from:-

Simon Blundell, Reform Club Librarian, who showed an interest and helped me find books in our extensive collection to which I hope this will add a small amount of credit.

The London Library, and especially the Trustees of the Carlyle Trust, for helping make it possible for a lowly paid public servant to be a member, I hope this will add to the knowledge in that institution

Michelle Alford in Hull City Libraries who bore with my witterings and vague requests for precise books, with steady determination and much tolerance.

Martin Taylor at Hull City Archives for pointing me in some good directions and just making available his general erudition, as well as his contacts.

The numerous staff at the National Archives who helped me out and explained the way round. There is a model of what a Public service should be, and the Staff there really do understand the concept.

The British Library. Where I write has an impact and I am grateful beyond measure to:-

The Trustees of the Gladstone Library, historically more properly St Deinol's for the accommodation and ability to just write in an air of contemplation and quiet discussions at meals. My family may have followed Chamberlain in the Home Rule divide but it was still a pleasure to be there and typical of Gladstone himself.

Dr Heseltine and the University of Hull for the generous opening hours of the BJ Library – so much longer now than when I was an undergraduate though alas, to my chagrin, it would probably have made little difference "back in the day"

The Principal of St Aidan's College Durham, again for a break so I could write – I shall cherish coming to breakfast and finding myself surrounded by middle-aged punk rockers up for a festival in Durham of all places! Only in England!

The Trustees of the "Lit and Phil," more properly the Literary and Philosophical Society in Newcastle upon Tyne for allowing me admission and again for a lovely place to write a book, and I hope the copy I will add to their centuries of supplying knowledge will help others too.

People I didn't meet but who helped:-

Deborah Bircham at Lincolnshire County Archives, who worked tirelessly to get me to see their collection, most usefully the notes of 617's Adjutant.

Peter Elliott, Senior Keeper, Department of Research & Information Services at the Royal Air Force Museum Hendon, who unlocked some RAF mysteries that must have seemed inane to him.

Chris Nathan, the archivist at St Edward's was kindness itself and selflessly passed me information, I hope this book will inspire some of the current schoolboys – although it was Gibson's own book that inspired me and still should stir schoolboys everywhere.

The National Archives of Canada Client Services Division who also bore with me (and discovered their catalogued item of a portrait of Gibson was not to be found) and my long-distance enquiries.

124

The Howard Hawks Collection is held as part of the L. Tom Perry Special Collections Library, at the Harold B. Lee Library in the Brigham Young University in Utah. I am grateful to them for furnishing me with a copy of the papers relating to the proposed Dambuster film

The Editorial Staff at "Britain At War" magazine who very kindly sent me a copy of their October 2011 issue.

The Staff at the Cornwall Archives and Libraries Service who helped me find information when I could not get there.

The people I owe on this journey are so many – if this is in your hands now it is because of all the experiences in my life that made me the person who could do it. However there are blazing beacons in the light of learning. Mrs Chevalier who first captured my attention in school lessons. My old history Master "Hugh" Aveling, who nurtured my love of History, and was one of the most inspirational classroom-educators I have ever met; as well as E.E. McCall who just persuaded me to go and read History at university as part of a Joint Honours. Mr Oddie I remember with affection for pastoral work when the term had not even been thought of by educationalists, and just failed to persuade me to read English at University – however I hope the fact I have written something will make amends. Also the Masters who said I would never succeed!

My colleague in the Ward John Abbott who, by doing his share of the task we have has restored to me my hinterland so I can do this.

The security staff at the BJ library for some chats in the library late at night and showing an interest in my work which sometimes helped clarify my thoughts.

The many friends who were there, and have always been there, when I stumble on the path of Life's Big Adventure: Christopher, Helena, Louise, Martin, Alan, Carl, Sean, Abi, John (all of them), Sarita, Dave, Karen, Kalvin, Tracey, Tracy, Nicola, Stuart, Neil, Paul, Claire – you know who you are I will not embarrass you or ruin your careers!

Rupert, my most tolerant of publishers all this stemmed from a casual aside on facebook and I am enormously grateful for a chance to do something fresh.

The proof-readers Irene, Charmaine, Nicci, Paul, Nicci's father (apparently), David. It always used to annoy me but now I see why people say it: all these people have been wonderful on this thrilling voyage, but they should not be blamed for any errors if made.

"You will deem it a proof of this pride of mine that I have prefaced [sic, in this precise case] these volumes with the names of my authorities. I have done so because it is, in my opinion, a pleasant thing and one that shows an honourable modesty, to own up to those who were the means of one's achievements"......Pliny The Elder

This is not a complete list but these were some of the most interesting books I used

Arthur, Max There Shall Be Wings The RAF from 1918 to the present Hodder & Stoughton London 1993

Arthur, Max, Dambusters, a landmark oral history Virgin, London, 2008

Bishop, Patrick Bomber Boys, fighting Back 1940 1945 Harper Press London 2007

Burke, Edmund Guy Gibson VC Arco 1961

Bowyer, Chaz Bomber Barons William Kimber London 1983

Boyle, Andrew No Passing Glory The full and authentic biography of Group Captain Cheshire VC, DSO, DFC Collins London 1955

Brickhill, Paul The Dam Busters Pan books London, 1954

Cooper, Alan The Men Who breached the dams, 617 Squadron the Dambusters William Kimber London 1982

Douhey, Guilio (trans Dino Ferrari) The command of the Air, Office of Air Force History, Washington 1983

Driesschen, Jan van den (with Eve Gibson) We Will Remember Them, Guy Gibson and the Dambusters Erskine, Norfolk, 2004

Euler, Helmuth (tr Michael Ockenden) The Dams Raid through the lens After The Battle London 2001

Falconer, Jonathan The Dam busters Story Sutton Publishing Stroud 2007

Frankland, Noble The Bombing offensive Against Germany, outlines and perspectives Faber & Faber London 1965

Galland, Adolf (trans. Mervyn Savill) The first and the last, the German fighter force in World War II Methuen London 1955

Garrett, Stephen Ethics and Airpower in World War II, the British Bombing of German Cities, St Martin's Press NY 1993

Gibson, Guy Enemy Coast Ahead

Gibson, Guy Enemy Coast Ahead – uncensored Crecy Manchester 2003

Goebbels, Joseph TageBucher, Band 4: 1940-1942 Piper, Munich 1992

Goebbels, Joseph TageBucher, Band 5: 1943-1945 Piper, Munich 1992

Goebbels, Joseph, The Goebbels Diaries (tr and ed Louis P. Lochner) Hamilton, London, 1948

Goebbels, Joseph, The Goebbels Diaries 1939-41 (tr & Ed Fred Taylor) Hamish Hamilton, London 1982

Grayling, A.C. Among the Dead Cities, was the allied bombing of civilians in WWII a necessity or a crime? Bloomsbury London 2006

Halpenny, Bruce Barrymore The Dambusters, "Lincolnshire Life" May 1981

Harris, Arthur Bomber Offensive Collins, London 1947

Hastings, Max Bomber Command Michael Joseph London 1979

Hinchcliffe, Peter Luftkrieg bie Nacht 1939-1945 Motorbuch Verlag, Stuttgart 1998

Jackson, Robert Before the storm, the story of Royal Air Force Bomber Command 1939-42 Arthur Barker, London 1972

Jacobsen, Hans-Adolf & Rohwer, Jurgen (tr Edward Fitzgerald) Decisive Battles of World War II, the German view Andre Deutsch London 1965

Knell, Hermann To destroy A City strategic bombings and its human consequences in World War II Da Capo Press Massachusetts 2003

Matthews, Rupert Heroes of Bomber Command - Lincolnshire Countryside Books, Newbury 2005

Moorhouse, Roger Berlin At war, life and death in Hitler's capital 1939-1945 Bodley Head, London 2010

Middlebrook, Martin & Everitt, Chris The Bomber Command War Diaries an operational reference book 1939-1945 Viking London 1985

Morris, Richard (With Colin Dobinson) Guy Gibson Viking 1994

Neillands, Robin, The Bomber War, Arthur Harris and the Allied Bomber Offensive 1939-1945 John Murray London 2001

Ottaway, Susan Dambuster The Life of Guy Gibson VC Pen and Sword 2007

Otter, Patrick, Lincolnshire Airfields in the Second World War Countryside Books, Newbury 1996

Pape, Robert A Bombing to Win, air power and coercion in war, Cornell University Press, 1996

Probert, Henry , Bomber Harris – his life and times Greenhill 2001

Ramsden, John The Dam Busters – a British Film Guide IB Taurus, London 2003

Richards, Denis & Saunders, Hilary St. George Royal Air Force 1939-1945 (3 vols) HMSO London 1954

Rumpf, Hans (tr Edward Fitzgerald) The Bombing of Germany Frederick Mueller London 1963

Saward, Dudley Bomber Harris – the authorised Biography Magna Print, Long Preston 1987

Speer, Albert, Inside the Third Reich (tr Richard and Clara Winston) Weidenfeld and Nicholson, London 1970

Sweetman, John The Dams Raid: Epic or Myth Operation Chastise Janes London 1982

Terraine, John The Right of The Line, the Royal Air Force in the European War 1939-1945 Hodder & Stoughton London 1985

Thacker, Toby Joseph Goebbels Life and Death Palgrave, Basingstoke, 2009

Thompson, Walter Lancaster to Berlin Totem, Toronto, 1987

Verrier, Anthony The Bomber offensive, B.T. Batsford 1968

Wilson, Kevin Bomber Boys, the Ruhr, the Dambusters and Bloody Berlin Cassell London 2006

Webster, Charles Sir & Frankland, Noble The Strategic Air Offensive Against Germany 1939-1945 4 vols HMSO London, 1961

OTHER SOURCES

Numerous papers at Kew after three weeks literally camping out. ORB for squadrons, stations, bases, Upkeep files, Submarine files, Chastise files, British dams, American visits, - smashing place.

RAF Various papers from The Royal Air Force Historical Society

Air Ministry. Bomber command : the Air ministry account of Bomber command's offensive against the Axis, September, 1939-July, 1941. HMSO London 1941

Air Ministry Bomber command continues : the Air ministry account of the rising offensive against Germany, July 1941-June 1942 / HMSO London 1942

Dictionary of National Biography 1941-1950 Oxford University Press 1959

The Journal of Modern History

Flight Magazine

Dambuster, Wing Commander Guy Gibson VC CD (ISBN 978-1- 906310-17-2)

www.Rafweb.org